A Hundred Journeys

Omar Zafarullah is a mechanical engineer with a degree from Yale University, Connecticut, USA, and is an executive in a Fortune 500 company. He belongs to Gojra and lives in Lahore. He regularly contributes articles to *The News*, the most-read daily in Pakistan. He is married to a doctor, Saira, and has two children, Hyder and Maya.

John + Caroline,

I hope you enjoy.

Omar Z.

A Hundred Journeys
~Stories of My Fatherland~

OMAR ZAFARULLAH

Published by
Rupa Publications India Pvt. Ltd 2017
7/16, Ansari Road, Daryaganj
New Delhi 110002

Sales Centres:
Allahabad Bengaluru Chennai
Hyderabad Jaipur Kathmandu
Kolkata Mumbai

Copyright © Omar Zafarullah 2017

This is a work of fiction. Names, characters, places and incidents are either the product of the author's imagination or are used fictitiously and any resemblance to any actual person, living or dead, events or locales is entirely coincidental.

No part of this publication may be reproduced, transmitted, or stored in a retrieval system, in any form or by any means, electronic, mechanical, photocopying, recording or otherwise, without the prior permission of the publisher.

ISBN: 978-81-291-4739-4

First impression 2017

10 9 8 7 6 5 4 3 2 1

The moral right of the author has been asserted.

Printed at Thomson Press India Ltd., Faridabad

This book is sold subject to the condition that it shall not, by way of trade or otherwise, be lent, resold, hired out, or otherwise circulated, without the publisher's prior consent, in any form of binding or cover other than that in which it is published.

To Maya

Contents

Prologue—A Letter ix

POLICY
The Canals 3
The Last Male 12
The First Jat 22

FAMILY
Three Births 29
The Last Mohican 30
Gojra 35
Mall Road 41
A Gathering Storm 44
The End of Time 47

A HUNDRED JOURNEYS
Hamid Pia 53
Needed, One Passport 64
World Cup 68
The World You Inherit 71
Rule Number 1 76
OutSource 81
Confidence 86

Robbery	88
Ninety-Seven Days	93
Love and God	97

WAR BY ANY OTHER NAME
Invasion	105
Waiting for Night to Fall	116
White Technologies	125
In Search of a Hero	136
Friendship	144
Naming the Taliban	146
End of a Movement	153

TRUST ME
Ten Days of School	163
Lessons from the War	166
Under a Darkened Moon	180
A Pious Bureaucrat	185
A Reason to Be	194

Prologue—A Letter

Dear Hyder,

I write in these few pages what I think you need to know. What I tell you is known to everyone in these parts but the effort it takes us to know what we know robs us of the energy to do what we must.

You will understand what I write when you are in your twenties. By then these words will not mean much—I hope.

We are at war. But we were not always at war. We have stumbled, but others have stumbled before us and recovered. Do not despair. We too will recover. And when we do, these words will tell you who we were and how you got here.

You know the basics. You know that my grandfather rose from the soil to become a doctor, and that my father was a judge who died when I was in school. You know I studied at Yale before trying my hand at business back in Pakistan—only to fail. You know that then I restarted, a new business again, from zero.

What you do not know is how the country too transformed around me and what I learnt along the way.

I hope I help you understand.

Your father

I
POLICY

The Canals

Policy is the enemy.

But it was not always the enemy.

A hundred years ago, one policy—a brilliant energy policy—pulled millions out of poverty.

Our family, whose holdings had shrivelled after generations of subdivision, also got a new lease of life.

My grandfather, the renowned Doctor Rehmatullah, born as this first energy revolution transformed the Punjab, was as old then as you are now.

In 1910, propelled by the invisible hands of policy, he and our entire family left Ropar to catch a train from Ambala Cantt into Lahore. And our story began. A second train took them to Lyallpur[*]. From there, bullock carts laden with lanterns, pots, beddings, unstitched cloth, ladles, wheat seeds, and followed by loyal dogs, they set off for Chak 480 along the banks of the majestic new Gogera Branch Canal, another few days' journey away.

And my grandfather clung to his mother as much as you do on your way to school.

He could not then understand the mighty forces, the

---

[*]Now Faisalabad.

bold engineering, the intricate financing that went into making his life change. He could only see the red-turbaned railwaymen in dusty loincloths, heaving huge rail tracks onto large wooden sleepers, placed evenly along a straight line of stone and macadam, emerging out of Lyallpur, heading towards his new home, along a new canal with freshly planted saplings equidistant and painted with chalk.

The land that today makes up the heartland of Pakistan was settled along rivers, leaving vast expanses to wilderness. British investment built barrages, dams and canals. Then they allotted these irrigated new lands, village by village, to residents of the lands settled earlier. A village on the banks of the Chenab would be allotted a new village of newly commanded land two hundred miles away. Water, which originated a hundred miles away, could now irrigate an acre of commanded land within one hour. This was equivalent to pushing five modern-day water tankers a distance of a hundred miles using oxen, only to irrigate one acre of land, once. No farmer could do this then or even now. Only a clever government, using long-term financial instruments, could engineer such a feat.

Amazing chances suddenly opened up for enterprising families to resurrect old fortunes, to seek new opportunities. Our family, too, was wide-eyed in expectation on arriving at their new home in Chak 480.

Chak 480, like all chaks designed by British planners, was a square village in the centre of a vast square of land subdivided into square plots distributed among the residents of the village. Each square of commanded land had two corresponding yards in the chak where villagers could make their homes. Our family arrived in their designated yard and began fashioning a house out of mud and straw.

Our family then, much as today, was full of young cousins and aunts, but there was one major difference. There was only one man in the family. All other adult men had died and the family was a patchwork of widows and orphans. My grandfather and his two elder brothers were the only lucky ones, not yet orphaned.

But there were enough young hands and animals available to build a neat little house out of straw and mud. More importantly, they began clearing their allotted plot of land of thorny shrubs and levelling the land with spades, and also started softening this land with the new miracle water that gushed from a regulated hole in the canal that was allowed to water each field for eight hours every week. As soon as the water seeped deep into the mud, and the land cooled and softened, cattle ploughs would begin turning it over. Whichever patch was left too high for the water to reach, was again levelled with a spade, and the process repeated with the next water cycle.

The spades used in the Punjab were designed for fashioning this hard, dry ground. They were not the straight spades with rounded tips used in the wet soils of Europe or East Asia to dig deep with each pushed stroke. Instead, they would only slice and scrape the earth every time they arced down to the ground, after being heaved over the farmer's head. The blade angled sharply back towards the handle and slashed through the earth more like a weapon than a tool. In millions of crude hands, these simple spades built the most sophisticated irrigation scheme on the planet, managed energy with incredible efficiency, and transformed my destiny—and yours.

It is amazing how a handful of planners in London and Lahore set in motion a policy that, on its own momentum, sucked millions of pounds and rupees across multiple banks and through countless hands, and forced salaried civil engineers and private contractors in an age-old embrace of ruthless execution that then extorted from the hands of millions of illiterate villagers—a back-breaking effort they gladly made, again and again. In the end, as barren land became lush and hopes rose nightly over hundreds of thousands of hot ovens, the money that had left with the strokes of bold pens, grudgingly but surely, returned to those banks as promised—in the shape of taxes.

A whole nation could now grow two crops in one year with less energy than their neighbours and, thus, could all enjoy a surplus to then spend or save according to need.

What a policy! A policy that invested in infrastructure that used energy more efficiently and made our lands more productive; a policy that allowed our family—effectively you and me—to rise out of poverty.

∞

Almost hundred years later, in 2005, I took my cousin's Honda Acura and pointed it north of New Jersey. Rolls of cut grass, all bigger than any tractor in Punjab, lay scattered on farms bigger than all the land of all the Jats in our village. New Jersey gave way to New York, and New York nudged up against Montreal.

Montreal came upon me without much fuss. We were not yet as frowned upon as we are now, and before I knew it, the signs were in French and the wind unrelenting.

Saeed Quraeshi was one of the top wind turbine designers of the world, with many records under his belt. Almost six-feet tall, with aquiline features and a distinguished bald head, he was a Pakistani, married to a French Canadian. His house was placed as if in Noddy's Toy Town, without a flake of snow amiss. It was warm, and scarves hung next to umbrellas and hats by the door.

We had been working together for a year, trying to bring his wind turbines to Pakistan. He wanted to do it for his country—to give the fruits of his international expertise back to his homeland. I wanted to do it because it seemed like a good idea and because his daughters were very pretty. He was a man obsessed with wind and aerodynamics, and I was fortunate to have him as a mentor. We had, in the previous year, spent many hours in his research office hunkered over the wind policy of Pakistan. We had reworked feasibilities and had pondered over airport wind data. But I had made that final trip to his home to explain to him that we had failed, that there was no way that we could put up his wind turbines in Pakistan. He kept countering with solutions, but I explained to him painfully what I am explaining to you now, that we were up against a monster. And the name of that monster was policy.

∞

Our energy policy came in glossy print and was advertised

on websites. But this policy did not make any decisions. It only assigned decision-making powers to different government departments—on a case-to-case basis.

It was forty pages long.

It sat in my bag and then on my desk and then on the window sill behind the curtain as we dipped from an energy surplus to an energy deficit while our neighbours—the ones we had beaten in decades past—kept adding megawatts and megawatts of cheaper and cheaper power to their arsenal.

I did not then know what was really wrong with our energy policy. But one day, much after the fact, I chanced upon the wind policy of the state of Gujarat, which lies in India. And I began to understand.

This document was only two pages long.

Those two simple pages signed by a mid-level government employee took amazing decisions. They decided the rate at which wind power would be bought by a utility company in that calendar year. They also decided the rent, in energy units, that the utility can charge to the wind farm in case the wind farm does not sell to the utility but to another user connected to the utility. And that was it.

The rest was then taken care of by businessmen—similar to the canal policy of a century ago.

The wind policy in Gujarat was announced about the same time as ours. Today, that state alone makes 3,000 megawatts of wind power.

On our side of the border, the sum result of our policy, fifteen years in, was that Pakistan was producing 3 megawatts of wind power and the powerful retirement fund of the military had extracted the right to sell wind power to the grid for the next ten years at twice the rate fixed in Gujarat.

∽

Unfortunately, energy makes the world go round.

From the Aryan hordes who first harnessed the compact energy of Central Asian horses, to the Dutch who ruled the globe through their mastery over wind energy, to the British who cracked the world open using the coal in Newcastle, to the Americans who extracted cheap oil from their vast plains, civilizations have suddenly become unbeatable when they cornered the market on the most flexible form of energy of the time.

∽

Our history too is best told in terms of energy.

We import our oil and we use our ability to harness nuclear energy not for electricity but for bombs.

We can afford to do so because we have now, for a century, become fat on the god-gifted energy of abundant water, luckily harnessed, first by British and then by our own engineers. This gave us an unbelievable edge over our neighbours to the east and to the west, who were forced to burn diesel to get the same water we received through gravity.

This allowed us to accumulate surplus wealth that a farmer in Afghanistan or Rajasthan could not hope to match.

This surplus was then used in astounding ways that have

today shaped Pakistan into an equally astounding country.

The first use we made of the surplus was to bring more and more acreage under cultivation. There was no need to optimize. So much water was available that adding acres was more cost effective than increasing yield.

The second use was in enticing population to grow. Every able hand could find work in a field and more hands meant more access to the plenty of this bountiful land.

The third—most oft-repeated—use was in building up a large army everyone hopes will save us one day.

The fourth use was in building up a very small minority of highly educated elitist professionals who have, in individual capacities, shone in their fields globally. This fourth use shows up in the most improbable places and forms on this planet—sometimes as a Nobel laureate, sometimes as an Olympic gold medallist, and sometimes as a nuclear bomb or a new wind turbine. Thus, we created what continues to astound the world—nuclear scientists and physicists in a sea of illiterate urban peasants.

But this surplus felt good.

We were richer than all our neighbours. We were the first to get television in the region. We built a refinery in Karachi before the Arabs built one in Arabia. We became the fittest population in the Middle East and South Asia. We were world champions in all the sports we played.

But then, twenty years ago, we stopped reinvesting in energy infrastructure.

Without investment, dams began to silt up, reducing their capacity and flexibility. A shortage of electricity forced us to focus on emergency solutions. When oil was cheap,

The Canals • 11

we bet on making power from this oil—a bet even the US could afford only in its prime. When oil prices rocketed this century, we moved the same power plants to gas, a resource on which we could place any price we wanted. Then the gas pipes too began creaking from the pressure and, finally, the economy tanked. Our surpluses disappeared. We first began to lose in hockey. And then also in cricket.

The Last Male

Despite the canals, we as a family would have been ground into the earth were it not for my great-grandmother. Her husband—my great-grandfather, the last adult male of the clan—died in a railroad accident before the first harvest, before even the complete taming of this new land was completed.

A clan of women and orphans was left with no time to mourn or sulk. The land granted by government fiat on a piece of paper no one had ever seen, quickly began to shrink. Other clans vied to take over and capture by force what was granted by law. As the other clans started their rise as landowners, our clan clung to a mud home and a subsistence-sized piece of land with my great-grandmother, Maaji, fiercely in charge.

Maaji was not much older than your mother today, Hyder, when she began to rebuild, season by season, oxen upon oxen. She tilled the land with wooden ploughs and marshalled her nieces and nephews and sons to stick together. She wore a black ghagra—a loose billowing skirt—on top of a long loose shirt and a cotton scarf against the sun. She fended against encroachers and wild animals with wooden sticks, and commanded in a voice so strong that when she shouted for one of her sons from the fields, she could be heard loud and clear in the village.

She did not remarry and she did not give up.

Remember to keep Maaji's picture in your mind whenever someone raises the schoolbook concept of purdah. Just remember that Islam is first and foremost for the downtrodden, and when you are downtrodden nobody will help you except yourself. And I cannot believe Islam would not allow Maaji and countless others like her to push their way out of poverty through honest hard work. The schoolbook concept of purdah takes away this right from women and I cannot therefore reconcile myself to it. It makes Islam an elitist religion, not practical for the poor who cannot afford purdah for practical economic reasons.

Remember that luckier families in the same village could afford for the women to stay at home and that these women would go to the fields at midday with hot rotis for their men. But Maaji would leave home at dawn and, together with her young sons, would work the fields more desperately than the neighbouring men because her family could not afford any mistakes. Her family had been robbed of its land by the same people who could afford to be complacent and comment that it was not a woman's place to work in the fields.

Remember too that she had to borrow and seek help from these same neighbours who were, after all, going back generations, our relatives. She could only afford to listen and fiercely nod at such comments because she was then sitting on the wrong side of time. But her blood boiled and that blood still connects us with that time and puts us forever at odds with that class of men who always had all the answers and to whom we must listen and nod because we have no choice.

Also remember that you are not the son of your father if your blood does not boil when you hear such comments. For today we as a family sit on the right side of time. We too have become lucky. We too have become junior members of the class of men who have all the answers.

Still, time is as cruel today as it was then. A handful of families on the right side of time still decide what is acceptable and what is not. Today not only have they co-opted schoolbook Islam into their arsenal, but have also perfected an anti-merit system that makes it more and more difficult for hardworking families on the wrong side to make a jump to the right side as we did.

Remember too that mere entry into this lucky group does not give you the authority or strength to influence the thinking of the lucky families, because the families who were lucky then—our neighbours from the past—have over time become so much more powerful and richer that their thoughts and their concepts of the world are now the dominant point of view in Pakistan. And as these people become your friends and the friends of your friends, remember again that they too have no way of knowing that they are wrong. You, like Maaji, will find yourself nodding in agreement to these people more often than you like. But, at least, remember.

Today, as I accompany clients on trips to the West or to the East, I sometimes hear comments stressing how lucky we are in Pakistan that our women still stay at home and how our society still has its bearings because of these women.

I do not have the moral courage to tell them how I really feel, for fear of losing business. Once, though, as I boarded a luxury bus at Islamabad, and a brave young hostess brought us some coke, the gentleman sitting next to me turned his head away in disgust. As soon as she moved away, he told me how wrong it was that such an act was being allowed in an Islamic country, that it was disgraceful that her brothers and father were living off her income. He told me that he had had the strength to marry off his two daughters even before they were sixteen because this was his duty and he was not greedy to wait for a rich son-in-law as most people do.

I listened for some time because it is always good to listen in order to understand. As I listened and nodded my head, he gained in confidence and in volume. I thought I would, over the next four hours, be able to understand this school of thought—enough to write about in a book perhaps. But then suddenly, without warning, my blood began to boil. I turned to him and spoke very very slowly, each word boring into his chest. I told him that if he uttered another word before we reached Lahore, I would break his legs and have him arrested for breaking the law, and if he could not stand to look at women working then he should stay at home. He did not say anything after that. I have never reacted so strongly to anything in my life, and I have had quite a life.

The future of your nation is in the hands of its women. They are brave and resourceful, and do not let anyone tell you differently. You, of all people, must know this because you would not be reading and I would not be writing had it not been for the strong women who fashioned the foundations of our family. I know such women even today, holding their families together in the face of seeming extinction.

∽

Once, as I sat in a masjid with one of my uncles in Gojra, our hometown, which still wears a shadow of Maaji in the evenings, and of my father and of his father at the height of noon, children played marbles outside in the alleyway and a preacher expounded on the changing state of women in our society. The preacher pointed to the teaching of geography, in schools, to impressionable women as an attempt by a heretic government to show women maps of adjoining areas, thus making it easier for them to elope. Most people in the congregation took this as a great joke, which was then repeated at countless lunches and family weddings, but no one, including myself, found it important enough to challenge the preacher or find a way to remove him from his position of authority.

That preacher's salary was paid by taxpayers and his appointment was made by an obscure department far away in Islamabad in an obscure office under the Ministry of Religious Affairs.

But the question of gender equality and purdah is not just a religious issue. In fact, if one has to resolve this anomaly in our society, it is important not to attack it on religious grounds, but instead to approach it from a practical angle.

Kaizen is a Japanese management tool now taught in all business schools for fixing big problems using simple steps. One amazing rule in Kaizen is that to find the root cause of any problem, you need to ask *why* every time a cause is discovered and to ask this at least six times before you can really get to the root cause.

So I decided to try Kaizen one day as I sat in a Honda car workshop in Islamabad. Incongruously, a female accountant sat in the office in this perfectly manly domain, punching away on her computer. I could not refrain from asking her why she was not wearing a purdah (or hijab). She told me that she had recently started wearing hijab on her way to the office and that she had taken it off once she was inside, but her parents were not happy with her wearing it at all. Her parents and all her aunts and uncles, she said, could not understand why she had to wear one because no one in their family had ever done so before.

'But perhaps women in your family never worked outside home before?' I asked.

'Exactly,' she said. 'They cannot understand.'

'But you are not wearing it here?' I asked.

She said there was no need. 'The buses are very congested in the rush hours,' she explained, 'and there is never enough space in the seats reserved for women.' She had found, like most of her friends, that boys did not bother her much if she wore a hijab. Besides, fighting for a space on those buses, I know personally, is not a job for the faint-hearted.

We were getting closer to Kaizen now with only three more *why*s to go. 'Why do you think the buses are so congested?' I asked her. She looked at me with eyes like daggers. I was mocking her. I was lucky that I could sit and ask these questions, she thought, and she had to answer them. But if she could, she would force me to spend the rest of my life commuting on the 'death-bullet' Toyota van that she was obliged to use every day, rather than a public bus provided to citizens—men and women—by every other nuclear-armed government in the world. She decided to tell me a story instead.

'When the British exiled the last Mughal emperor of India to Burma,' she said, 'they put him in a cell only five-foot high. Do you know why?' She turned the questioning back to me, putting her pen down in triumph. 'Because they never wanted him to hold his head high, ever again. The Toyota HiAce,' she told me conspiratorially, 'is also a design perfected to subjugate your mind and body. You must always bend down to enter its confined space and you will remain bent when you eventually squeeze your frame out of it. If you ride it every day, you will never raise your head in freedom again,' she said, as only an employee of Honda could.

That was all the Kaizen I could handle.

This young woman felt secure in the home governed by her father and in the office governed by a Pakistani businessman, but not in the city governed by the Government of Pakistan. If she could have good transport and a feeling of security, she would have chosen to dress pretty much like Maaji—as secure in the home as on the fields. And if such security and such services were provided to all girls, fathers would not hesitate to send their daughters out for work, suddenly increasing the productivity of the nation. When public goods like security and transport are not available, families are forced to spend their private resources to provide them. Many brothers spend hours every day ferrying their sisters to colleges or to their jobs and then back again—at tremendous cost to their own and the nation's productivity. For an average urban family with one girl, this lack of decent services effectively means a tax of approximately two hundred and forty dollars per year. Now, if this problem afflicts one in two families in a city such as Lahore, a good transport infrastructure in Lahore would effectively erase this tax from all of these families, putting an extra three hundred million dollars into the hands of Lahoris *every year*, without even accounting for all the women who would now be able to work and generate multiples of this amount in added productive capacity.

∽

One of my cousins, Hamid Pia's elder brother, a doctor in Pakistan, is married to a doctor and has three lovely daughters. When both the parents went out to work, they would lock their house from the outside and instruct the girls, then in their teens, to not open the door unless they received a confirming knock that served as a secret password between the parents and their children. The girls were barricaded not for religious or cultural reasons. They were barricaded because security cannot be guaranteed in our cities. And if one was to attempt the rescue of these girls from this seclusion, one cannot argue with preachers sitting on pulpits, but with government policies and budget allocations and with the fabric of autocratic rule that did not allow my cousin to get together with his neighbours and arrange for his colony to elect an honest police chief and a judge with credibility.

One day my cousin arrived to say goodbye. His emigration papers for America had arrived after fifteen years of processing. But despite everything he did not want to leave. He did not wish to leave the land of his youth and of his loves and of his ancestors. That day we cried to a man, all my cousins, as we packed him off to the new world with his wife and three daughters.

A week later, all three girls were going to school free of cost on a school bus paid for by the county of Lake Hiawatha in New Jersey. My cousin had tears in his eyes when after a month he sat on his porch and saw his daughters cycling around his new colony free, as all children should be. He knew that his daughters could have never had this opportunity in Pakistan and that sadly he had finally come home.

∞

But, to complete our Kaizen journey, we must again ask why. Why is it that good security and transport infrastructure are not there and will not be there unless you and I put our heads together?

Lahore, which has a population equal to that of Switzerland, has one of the best transport systems in Pakistan. Roads are not as congested as in Delhi and the air is not as polluted as in Mexico City. But if you look at public transport, you will realize that it gets attention only during democratic rule. When I was growing up in the Zia dictatorship, beige Volvo buses, at the very ends of their mechanical lives, used to travel back and forth on these roads. From their vintage, one could judge that these had been ordered and put into use by an earlier democratic government, but during the eleven years of Zia's dictatorship no reinvestment had been made in the sector. Toyota HiAce vans had thus become the only feasible option by the time democracy again took root. Under democracy, a new bussing scheme was launched on the major routes of the city and one could, with dignity, board a bus from one part of Lahore and get off at the other with ego intact. During General Musharraf's martial law, though, these simple services suffered yet again.

Today we again have democratic rule.

We again have a chance to rebuild. To take back the years lost and reinvest in our women—in dignified transportation, in common sense security.

The First Jat

We are Jats. Jats are landholding wheat growers. We are known for strength and for a hearty appetite, but not for our studies.

When I was in school, my physics teacher once took me aside to question me about a mystery that had troubled him since he had begun teaching me. He said that he had seen many Jats come and go. He had seen football players, hockey captains, good boys, but none before me who was a good student. He said he could not decipher this mystery and I said I could not either because I had never known of such a mystery. But I remember asking my father this question when I got home.

And he told me that Jats, because they own land, had never felt the need to study hard to make a living. For them, the produce from the land was the only way to make a living. 'But then, what about us?' I asked him. 'Why are we then different?'

'Because we had almost no land,' he said. He told me that we would not have survived had we not been schooled. He told me the story of his father, whose father—Maaji's husband—had died in a rail accident in the crossing to the new lands and whose mother tilled the little land they still commanded. Thus, the whole family toiled while the youngest went to school. My father, me, you and our whole clan would still be toiling in others' fields, fighting over scraps of land, had it not been for this crucial decision and had it not been for the high-quality school operated by the British Raj in our small village.

This village school not only prepared my grandfather for life, it also gave him a scholarship, on merit. The primary school was replaced by a secondary school in Samundri, a walk of ten miles and then by a high school in Gojra, a bike ride of two hours. At each step, my father's father kept receiving scholarships from the British Raj and at each step this scholarship gave our family the required impetus to keep him in school.

There were countless moments when the education in hand could have landed him a job, allowing the family to cash in its investment in education, but they kept going and he kept going to school. After clearing eighth grade, he was offered a teaching job in the village school. Refusing, he carried on with his studies. But as he cleared his tenth, he was again offered a teaching job, this time in Samundri, which he proudly accepted only to be given a sound beating by his elder brother for giving up too early. So he went back to studying instead.

He would remember till his dying day a vision of his mother as she arrived to meet him, one lonely evening, as he sat in the verandah of the Gojra High School, unable to make it back to his village that night because the exam had finished too late. There was no way to go back home. And there was no way anyone could have come from the village.

But then he saw the unlikeliest of images: his mother, sitting on the back of a gypsy bullock cart, her ghagra tossing with the wind, leading a caravan to the gates of his school. Her dupatta swaddled a roll of roti with some blocks of gurr, and she held it to her chest as if the treasures of Solomon were wrapped in that one cloth. She thanked the gypsies for the ride, and, alone, mother and son spent the night in the verandah of the high school.

My grandfather wept like a baby when he himself was as old as a tree when he recalled his mother and that image—at once forlorn and majestic—is now seared into the memory of all his descendants.

For we would not be we, were it not for that singular struggle against ignominy, that young mother's belief in a set of books she could not herself read.

And then the day arrived when the family sent their son, the father of my father, to Amritsar for an interview for admission to Glancy Medical College. Again, the family put all their savings in his young hands to buy some good clothes for the task at hand. Until that point he had never worn Western clothes, which he needed for the interview. On arriving in Amritsar he realized that the money in his pocket could either get him a pair of trousers or a pair of boots. With the gentle Amritsari evening falling on his peasant shoulders, he decided on the trousers. Keeping just enough money in hand to buy a rail ticket home, he curled up in a corner of a mosque for the night, the money folded into a roti, the roti folded into a cloth, the cloth folded into his hands, his hands folded under his body, his body snuggled under his unfurled turban.

The next morning, he pulled his head through his billowing peasant tunic and tucked the tunic into his new trousers, without a belt. He again tightened his turban atop his head and then, put on his well-worn desi slippers. The slippers were covered in embroidered flowers sewn into the leather with metal wire so minutely that the leather was hidden from view and impossible to polish. He did not own socks.

As he sat in the waiting room outside the principal's office with the other candidates, who had come from all the top cities of the Punjab, he could see felt hats and two-tone shoes and double-breasted suits and silk handkerchiefs and double-eyed suspenders and starched shirts with stiff collars. But he could not note their import; he saw only that everyone wore socks and that all the shoes had laces.

When he was called in for his interview and entered, all skin and no sock, the principal was shocked to learn that this was Rehmatullah, the boy who had topped the exams in a region that stretched from Delhi to Peshawar. The principal awarded him not only admission but also a scholarship and a stipend.

Rehmatullah would become a doctor, one of the most famous eye surgeons of his time. The tough times slowly ebbed away and my grandfather became a pillar for the entire family, but he never forgot his brothers, who sacrificed their youths so he could be what they could not.

And we became a family on the right side of history, a family of Jats who liked to go to school because we had no other choice.

II
FAMILY

Three Births

I was born in 1971, to Zafarullah, the fourth son of Doctor Rehmatullah, the year when Pakistan was cleaved into two parts. So today's Pakistan, today's Bangladesh and your father were all born the same year.

The significance of 1971 is hard to explain. It is not polite to talk about it and you will have to read up on it yourself without help from your teachers.

Also in 1971, both parts of the cleaved country were suddenly delivered into the unprepared hands of their shocked civilian populations. It was a tumultuous year.

But I will not trouble you with more than you need to know right now. I will tell you more, later—much later—when you are ready to listen. For you cannot understand fully 1971 until you understand fully Pakistan.

The Last Mohican

My uncle, Chachoo Jaidee, was the quintessential Mohican of his time. He was my father's youngest brother, the seventh son of Doctor Rehmatullah and the last of a dying breed of men who populated these parts in the second half of the last century.

He cut a handsome figure on his Yamaha 50 with his fuddy-duddies and his flying shoes, which zipped up rather than laced down. He logged solo hours at the Flying Club and devastated co-eds at Punjab University with his dashing quietude, punctuating his silences with puffs on his Rothmans King Size.

His friends came in all shapes and sizes, and never left. He was their leader, though he never once acted like the leader. One friend was fatter than Chachoo, one was darker than Chachoo and one was less worldly than Chachoo, but they were all intensely loyal to him. Such loyalty was enjoyed by all Mohicans. It stems initially from the hidden admiration that men feel for those among them who can attract female attention. But such admiration would soon turn into envious hatred were it not for the second most Mohican of traits, a most sincere and even-handed cold shoulder to all affected females. This was the essence of

Chachoo's storied love life, which is easily a yardstick for Mohican genes: boy sees girl, boy puffs on Rothmans, girl sees boy, boy peers through smoke, boy thinks sorrowful thoughts, girl is moved, boy goes home on Yamaha.

Yet there were stories.

The script of these stories never veered from these basics, but the moment you walked into his room, you became the audience, and the friend would narrate to you a story about Chachoo. Chachoo would shake his head and scrape molten wax from a candle's edge back into its flame, while the rest of us would slowly begin to trundle in our minds onto the night train to Baluchistan.

As the train escapes Punjab and starts to cut across lonely rock faces, the night sky comes alive with stars, and everyone in the rail carriage drifts into sleep. It is by happy coincidence that the narrator is awoken in the middle of the night to witness a scene he will never forget and the audience grows ever-impatient to find out. The narrator paints a bleary-eyed picture of college students slumbering in every corner of the airy carriage. He notices the colour of the sky and the direction of the moon and a lissom figure stretched wantingly over canvas luggage rolls, with a book open to the moon and her tresses heaving with the wind. But her eyes, he clearly sees, are not on the book. They are on another shadow that sits on a berth, identified by the glowing tip of his cigarette.

The narrator pauses.

The room can think only one thought—Rothmans King Size.

The narrator snakes his breathless story through panicky

dark tunnels and then to wet shoes on a sunny lake and to picnics where sandwiches are offered with trembling hands, but the two main actors never really move from their original separate perches, connected through the eyes but separated by a heroic silence like two characters out of a PTV long play.

Thus, on endlessly hot summer afternoons or on chilly November nights I could simply open a door and enter a room with an ever-changing canvas—in the middle of a conversation or of a card game—and assist in rebuilding a carburettor or understand how the Left was different from the Right or work on a jigsaw puzzle. All by opening a single door.

Chachoo Jaidee, as I said, was my father's youngest brother. He lived with us and he would, after an episode of *Starsky and Hutch*, slowly explain to us how only an American car could take such pounding and how a Japanese car would have simply given in at the shocks on the first jump. He told the history of recent civilizations through their automobiles. He could explain everything rationally but slowly. He explained military coups and village politics. He would stare at a VCR's internals, for hours. And we were welcome to stare with him.

He was the last of the Mohicans, the last of Pakistan's Mohicans.

One such night, as autumn stretched into winter and the chill wind of Baluchistan thundered into Punjab, my cousin Zayn and I fought over a quilt while playing a game of rummy with Chachoo Jaidee. The topic was death. Chachoo explained how it made religion necessary. The lights were cut, a storm was pending. A candle lit the room.

A light knock on the window, like the rapping of a squirrel. We ignored it at first, but the knock was persistent. Chachoo placed his cigarette in the lip of the ash tray, reassembled the folds of his woollen shawl, and slid back the curtain. The window was dark but the rapping continued. As we tried to peer through the dark, a clap of lightning suddenly lit up the trees outside and we saw it, the grinning head of Qamar Din, framed perfectly by the four edges of the window pane. Qamar Din was our cook and he was the anti-Mohican.

He was a foot shorter and a hundred pounds lighter than his wife. In his lifetime of cooking, his hands had become immune to heat and all his fingers looked like thumbs he would plunge with ease into a fire to retrieve a perfectly cooked roti. No one knew what his head looked like because he never took off his woollen cap, even in summer. When he went to the bazaar, the kids of the area would scream, 'Smell is here!' But he had a power over women that was legendary. Some thought it came from a stash of cash he had buried somewhere in the ground. Others thought otherwise. But somehow he managed to keep finding mistresses half his age, again and again, despite having a grinning face that was the last thing you wanted to see in a flash of lightning on a stormy night.

He purred excitedly with news that our milk buffalo was unable to fully breathe and was tossing its last breaths. It had to be slaughtered—before it died. That much was clear. But Qamar Din needed Chachoo Jaidee to hold the decision and the knife in his own hands. And then he disappeared as swiftly as he had arrived.

It was a wild and stormy night. We could now begin to decipher from the howling of the wind and the thrashing of the branches, the stunted scowls of a thrashing beast. Chachoo Jaidee could not bring himself to order the execution of such a fine animal, yet he could also not bear to listen to its agonizing throes. This was not what he was designed for. Nor was I. But Zayn was built of other matter. He understood quickly that this was not a chore for the faint-hearted. He retrieved his slippers from under the bed and strutted into the night. There, under a huge, hundred-year-old tree, he saw the black animal convulsing, men with ropes pulling at each limb. He was handed a knife.

It was a bread knife, the biggest knife in Qamar Din's kitchen. But it was not designed to cut into flesh. It could only tear at the animal's thick skin with each shove from Zayn's hand. When Zayn's hand grew tired, he handed the knife back to Qamar Din, and the two of them waged a war of attrition all night, while Chachoo Jaidee died with each passing minute until finally, with the first light, the battle was won. And the beast and Chachoo Jaidee each crumpled into a silent heap.

Zayn is my cousin, but he is more of a younger brother. We lived in the same house and shared the same room until I left for college. Zayn joined the Army.

Gojra

You are cousins. Brothers. When you enter the house of a brother you must never open the door with your hand. You must kick it open with your leg. And demand, 'Chachi, roti'.
—Taya Latif, third son of Doctor Rehmatullah

Finding a girl for Chachoo Jaidee was almost as difficult as it was, a generation later, to find a girl for me. Chachoo Jaidee's career path, just as mine a generation later, was not possible to define in linear terms. And fathers-in-law prefer linear equations. Was Chachoo Jaidee a pilot or was he a lawyer? How could he be both? But he was. And there was the question of sociology. It was clear that he had a degree in that as well. And for those who knew, at the bottom of a black leather satchel that sat atop his galvanized iron closet was a stack of poems he had penned between puffs taken on his Rothmans King Size.

The case of Chachoo Jaidee would open every time the family gathered in Gojra.

Three sisters and six sisters-in-law, relieved of their duties as mothers and homemakers now that they were in the house of my grandfather Doctor Rehmatullah, would gather on the broad verandah overlooking the bricked courtyard and would needle Chachoo Jaidee.

'Our boy is so handsome. Who would not want our boy?'

'The hair has started to thin, but a broad forehead is becoming in a man.'

And Chachoo Jaidee would lean against the red-polished cement of the pillars that hid him from us as we battled instead in the bricked courtyard with hockey sticks and a ball.

'But a man must have a girl.'

'Na but what if he does not like girls?'

And suddenly pandemonium would break loose. Charpoys would heave back and forth as women hid behind cushions and chadors and someone would look for an imaginary sandal as unfettered joy would rock the house at such naughtiness until everyone's catharsis was complete. Then, still catching their breaths, the charpoy-ship would change tack.

'No, no, he likes girls. Didn't you see him craning his neck when Bubbo from Hafizabad was dancing at Guddi's wedding?'

'Leave ji. That time even Taya-ji stopped talking. They all wanted to look. They are all the same.'

'Haan then, you remember when Gul came to meet Khala-ji and she needed a ride to the station, and Jaidee wanted to drive her all the way to Gujranwala?'

'Leave Gujranwala ji. Our boy is not made for Gujranwala.'

'Na then, what is he made for?'

'Jaidee, tell us.'

'No leave, tell us. What are you made for?'

Chachoo Jaidee would answer with an enigmatic smile that encouraged further banter.

All this while a cork ball, bereft of all colour, would rocket across the bricks, through a few potted plants, between an electric motor and its pump, and a constantly changing cast of about a dozen players—all dressed in shalwar kameez and all drenched in each other's sweat. To someone not of the family, all these players would look the same—all grandsons of Doctor Rehmatullah—but for us each face was a novel, a story to be told.

There was the first-born, who was expected to lay the foundations of a nation-state, but whose voice would break as he recited to us the poems of Iqbal. There was the second-born, who could wrestle a buffalo and star in an Italian western. There was the middle-born, who would invariably throw his hockey stick into a wall before the end of a losing match. There was the constantly jilted Romeo, who would only keep goal. There was the acrobat, who was more interested in lighting firecrackers than the game. There was the stubborn one, who could eat a dozen rotis to win a bet but who could also play a flute with such sweet melancholy that it melted hearts across multiple courtyards. There was the quietly introspective one, who travelled with a book and came out of a match with the crease on his starched shalwar unruffled. There was the one who could jump on a hand grenade to save you and would cycle to Faisalabad for chicken tikka, but would never climb the verandah's cement shade to retrieve a ball. There was the one who would forgo a goal if you asked nicely, but would go nuts if you cheated. There was the always-smiling one, who would be anything you wanted him to be: goalie, defender, right-out, left-in or water boy. There was one, Hamid Pia, who only played because it was necessary. Then there were those who were younger. They did not matter.

You see, age mattered. We knew every nuance, story and preference of those who were elder to us. In every group, you always knew who was the youngest because he would have to leave his seat or get water or shuffle the cards and the others could relax in their seniority. Hockey teams were always distributed according to age. The oldest two were captains and they chose not according to ability but according to age.

They also decided the rules of the game, which for the more imaginative would devolve into complex hide-and-seek and then into pitched battles using the small inedible lasoora fruit of the trees in the hospital's waiting area. All strategies were game. Some would try to corner access to the lasoora trees—thus cutting off access to ammunition. Some would take a few projectiles in their pocket and sit quietly on a wall, waiting for the others to lose patience and finally come out of their hiding places to get pummelled. Others would blitz the competition in thunderous raids. Hamid Pia and I would plan ahead. Every year we would sneak up into the trees at night and hoard dried fruit in paper bags that we would hide in the ventilation windows on the roof of the house and would dip into this hoard every time the others ran to the trees.

The way we negotiated our changing positions through, against or with each other on that brick courtyard in Gojra trained us for life and connected us in an unspoken bond you now call family.

But those changing negotiations were so tantalizing that we had no idea great happenings were taking place as we kept trying to dodge each other into exhaustion. Our fathers, the sons of Doctor Rehmatullah, would sit in the cool room over unending cups of tea and glasses of lassi, and go on long walks together, and in these discussions they would decide somehow on matters of the family.

We discovered one day, while we were busy converting our hockey team into a cricket team, that the whole family—apart from us boys—was missing, and that Chachoo Jaidee had not shaved. And then evening fell and the whole clan returned in very high spirits. It turned out that Chachoo Jaidee was now engaged. It was not a surprise to us that we were not considered worthy guests for his engagement ceremony, but it was also not a surprise that even Chachoo Jaidee was not considered appropriate to attend his own engagement. My father rushed to a photo shop to get the photos of the ceremony developed so Chachoo Jaidee and everyone else could see the photos of our new Chachi.

∞

If, some August morning, you find yourself without a father and want to go home and smell the crackle of a roti as it comes out of the fire and rest your head awhile on a familiar shoulder, then knock the door of a Rehmatullah; in London, or Paris, or New York, or Dubai, or Karachi, or Lahore, or Gojra. Knock on the door and tell them the name of your father and the name of your grandfather and his father before him, and you will find what you seek. And do not open the door with your hand. Kick it open with your leg and demand loud and clear, 'Chachi, roti.'

Mall Road

A<small>LL</small> things of consequence happened on Mall Road. If it did not happen on Mall Road, it had no consequence.

You got a fountain pen at Anarkali, on Mall Road. You bought books at Feroze Sons, on Mall Road. Lawrence Garden, the Zoo, the Museum, the Secretariat, the Assembly building, Bank Square, my school, my father's court room, everything of consequence was on Mall Road.

When Benazir Bhutto first returned, she too arrived via Mall Road.

And what an arrival that was.

PTV did not cover it, but everyone knew she had arrived, and the Mall reverberated with drums and music, and dark wiry men without shirts and red and black bandanas danced with cathartic abandon as her truck laden with party workers kept moving the dancing boys forward and people hung from trees and clambered upon poles to get a first-look of this young woman that everyone seemed to know even though PTV had till then, in my consciousness, never mentioned her name. The aroma was more lentil, less meat, the broth was more water than vegetable, but the dish she now presented before us was very Lahori and most Pakistani. The boys who cavorted and screamed were all on the wrong side of time, but those who stood to the sides and peered—from the right side of time—also could not suppress a sudden glee, an improbable hope that we were, maybe, at some level, one.

My father brought a chair for his father, and placed it on a side street from where he could sit and see the tall passing truck of Benazir without getting crushed, but he allowed the rest of us to find our own perches and observe history as it began to turn once again in its slow arc towards democracy. I sat on a wall with Zayn. Had we known then, what we know now, that that homecoming was the greatest welcome put out by Lahore—ever—we would have paid more attention. Our eyes tried to focus not on Benazir but on the car right behind her truck. We could not believe what we were seeing.

Benazir's procession was long—many cars and vans and jeeps were following her truck. But we kept looking at the car just behind it. It was a white Nissan Sunny with two huge speakers mounted on its roof. We both knew the driver of this car. It was Nawaz, my grandfather's driver. And the car, if one disregarded the huge speakers mounted on the roof, looked suspiciously like my grandfather's car. Zayn and I looked at each other but could not speak in the absolute din of the best party ever.

Then, as the truck passed, Chachoo Jaidee signalled us and we went home for some tea and dinner and for news—which came from Chachoo's friends who kept moving with the procession, and when we knew, on the other side of midnight, that her procession had started nearing the Railway Stadium, we too piled on Chachoo's Yamaha 50 and got to the arena.

The stadium was lit with cheap yellow light bulbs strung awkwardly and its seats were cement but free and happy as it reverberated with forbidden music and outlaw poetry. Roasted daal in a cone of paper with a squeeze of lemon and a rollicking of pepper was the snack to have and a crate of coke in glass bottles would arrive next to you in anticipation of the thirst that always follows the spiced up daal. This was a rock concert of the Pakistani kind and then, like all rock concerts, the master of ceremonies announced and all eyes were glued to a distant gate which he announced would open and Benazir—now in a jeep—would drive into the stadium.

The gate opened and one could sense, through its sudden lurch, the pressure of humanity on the other side of the gate as party workers tumbled with the jeep onto the grass and organizers pushed and pushed the gate shut until finally, Benazir's jeep and one white Nissan Sunny with speakers on its roof, its bumper magnetically linked to the bumper of Benazir's jeep, squeezed into the stadium. Two vehicles made a stately procession to the stage. Benazir got off from the first. Nawaz got off from the second.

A Gathering Storm

I write because I need you to know what I cannot say.

I write about the past, about family, about country, because they all speak to me about my father, about Abu, and you need to know about him to know who you are, but I cannot bring myself to talk about him. He is one subject we do not talk about, because I cannot talk about him without my voice breaking. So I do not talk about him. It seems that I cannot write about him either, but you must understand: almost everything reminds me of him.

Chachoo Jaidee's broad shoulders ensconced in a light crumpled kurta, Taya-ji Latif's crackling voice, my sister's song, Zayn's flat down-the-line forehand, Hamid Pia's constant humour…everyone in my family reminds me of him.

When I rub soap in my face I remember the 7.30 a.m. All India Radio that would accompany his shave. When I wear my shoes I can hear how the tassels on his laces would hit the black leather of his oxfords in a strict staccato as he tightened the knot the same way every day. When I throw my trousers in a heap I remember how he would immaculately fold his Marks & Spencer wrinkle-free polyesters on a hanger, and every other week wash them himself and then hang them in the tub to make sure they would last and last.

I am not him just as you are not me. But that is all right. It does not mean that we are not connected.

When you asked me how long it takes to get to the moon, I told you three days because that is what he had told me. When you asked me what a clutch does, I could answer because I remember when I panicked and could not press the clutch and the car would not stop, and he pulled the hand brake, and we lurched almost into a tree, and then he laughed it off as I sat trembling.

My father could be every man. He could be a lowly farm-boy when talking to villagers and he could be a sophisticated legal expert when talking with city folk. He could play cricket with teenagers and he could talk for hours with retiring grannies. He was the life of any party.

Yet he did not tell me whether God exists. He did not tell me, or anyone else, why he began to pray in his forties. If asked, his stock response came with a twinkling smile: 'Just in case!' And yet he did not fast more than a few days every Ramadan and he would have his lunch in the judges' common dining room during the month. This is the reason my findings too on the subject are inconclusive.

Abu decided more cases in a day than some judges decided in a year, and yet he was polite and unhurried in his manner. The reason was preparation. He would, when we went to sleep, read all the case files for the next day and be ready for the lawyers, with crisp questions, in the morning.

With an LLM from Harvard Law School, grounded in the basics of the Pakistani system, he was a Jat from the middle of the Punjab, he was popular in the Bar. He was a gathering storm.

But I only know this now.

Then, I only knew him as a man who would rather do today what he could also do tomorrow. He would interrupt a shower to break a stick from the garden and unclog the gutter himself rather than wait for a plumber. In a family wedding, he would first make sure his father had eaten before he himself did but he would also be the first to dance.

Like you, he was full of energy. He saw in his work the worst and the best that our nation had to offer without any filters, and he kept moving on. For that is what we must do. He saw every day how the bullock cart and the fighter jet jostled for the same space in a country that needed room for both and he could reconcile centuries of tradition and thousands of years of technological bustle all on the same roads and yet was bold enough to continually speed forward. Where I become hesitant in the face of such choices, Abu was carefree in forging ahead.

Wrong choices made, he thought, are better than right choices not made.

The End of Time

Summer. August. 1986. A black Mazda zoomed across the Punjab plains. Abu, in a light blue kurta, was at the wheel. My mother, Ami, was in the passenger seat. My sister and I sat in the back. An assiduous forest officer a generation ago had planted kikar trees along this single-metalled road that led from the ancient city of Multan to the modern Air Force encampment in Shorkot. From here the road would turn to Jhang and then we would take the small track to Gojra, the town where our story began.

No one spoke as the stereo cassette player churned out the unmistakable voice of Abida Perveen:

The head of Mansoor,
Atop a spear,
Repeated:
I am God!
I am God!
I am God!

Shadows lengthened as the sun neared a spear's length from the horizon. Fields on all sides, having just borne a surplus of wheat, were lying in want of another crop.

Men like me and Abu sat far away in the shade of tali trees, waiting for the buffaloes as they splashed in village ponds. Others, more eager, were already shooing their buffaloes out of the water to get home to milk and then to sleep. These buffaloes would walk along the shoulder of the road caked in drying mud.

The mood in our car was also caked in tension. The country was ruled by a dictator. And Ami's brother had just been jailed for protesting against the general.

The road was clear when one of the buffaloes turned and stood in the middle of the road.

Seat belts were at the time classified as accessories and doubled the import duty, so few, if any, cars had seat belts. I was thrown forward as Abu jammed on the brakes. The car did not screech as the beast became bigger and bigger until it stood before us like a muddied black tank, the gristle on its underbelly about to be scooped up by our fender. But then Abu swerved right and we came to a stop alongside the beast.

The white Corolla approaching us from the opposite direction was still the size of a matchbox when we swerved and came to a stop in its path.

Abu pressed the accelerator again. But he forgot to press the clutch and the engine knocked before conking out.

The Corolla's grill was now visible. It was an '82. Abu turned the key in the ignition and the engine came alive. He quickly released the clutch only to realize that the gear was not in first. The engine knocked again but did not die. There was time only to press the clutch, move the gear out of fourth and into first.

That was all the time there was. I sensed panic in my father's hand.

The Corolla heaved, the front end coming down as the brakes were applied. The two cars came together, almost softly, like aluminium foil crushed together.

And that was that.

Soon I sat on a hospital trolley with bones broken, caked in blood, my brain in hyper drive, waiting. A frantic young doctor told me then that Abu had died. Ami and my sister Zara lay unconscious a few feet away. A strange old woman swatted flies away from my wounds. I cannot forget the policeman's desire to slap me for not telling him correctly the name of my tribe, my people, my qaum, and my displaced desire to explain to him how my qaum was no business of the state and if it was, my qaum was the same as that of Jinnah—I was a Pakistani. My qaum was Pakistan.

∞

When the rain first hits the Punjab, a million cravings spring forth.

You breathe earth in summer, but then when the heaving drops first melt the ground, you begin to *smell* the earth— and you stop.

You stop if you are making tea, you stop if you are milking buffalo. You stop if you are cutting metal.

You stop and feel the first heavy drops on your skin, and the dust and the summer walk away.

After a long long breath, life starts anew.

∞

A hundred different journeys began that night, all headed for Gojra as Jats and lawyers and bureaucrats and old tennis players got the news. But I began my journey out of Gojra, leaving the body of my father in the milling brick courtyard of his father, in a rickety ambulance with my sister on a stretcher in the back. It was, sadly, a happy starlit night for it was the night the first drops of rain hit the ground. But we did not stop. The ambulance cradled us through the magically flat plains of the Five Rivers as the Punjab stirred with the comings of the monsoon. Young boys checked roofs for imaginary leaks and young women paced their courtyards, looking for imaginary clothes hung out to dry.

When we entered Lahore it was morning, and the ambulance jostled with girls arriving for college and busy bodies munching on morning toast with jam. Lahore had stopped the previous night for the first drops of rain, but it was not about to stop for me. The world may have changed that last evening on a road on the way to Gojra. But the world was not going to stop.

III
A HUNDRED JOURNEYS

Hamid Pia

'Juhi Chawla in hot pants?'

'Juhi Chawla in hot pants.'

'Juhi Chawla in hot pants?' I repeated again, incredulous.

'Yes,' my cousin Hamid said softly, putting a hand on my shoulder. 'Juhi Chawla in hot pants.' Juhi Chawla. Miss India 1984, actress. Juhi Chawla, in hot pants.

'But...maybe you were mistaken, maybe someone else was...'

'No...no...no mistakes.' Hamid Pia looked into the distance and absent-mindedly dodged a traffic light with a stoop of his long neck. 'I saw it myself.' He had had a day to absorb the news.

'But...she could not...'

'Yes, she did.'

'Herself?' I needed time.

'Herself.'

'Why, Juhi... Why?'

We both swayed in silence.

∽

Hamid Pia and I never wandered the city aimlessly. Our

wanderings always had a mission. That day we were on a mission to buy a car. The mission had failed for now, but that did not deter us. We had read in the morning about an auction of government cars in the newspaper and had set out to try our luck. We would share the car. We were not deterred by the fact that no one our age owned a car or that we were not yet old enough to drive or that we were not legally allowed to get a car registered in our name or that there was no money in our pockets.

We had made it to the cricket ground next to the Secretariat and we had inspected all the worst-looking cars with care. It seemed like a day well spent. Then we had trudged back to the Mall and clambered to the roof of a beige Volvo bus.

The roof of a bus in slow-moving traffic is often a good place for reflection and confession.

I explained to Hamid Pia that the Secretariat was housed in the barracks of the French battalion that had once guarded Lahore against the British and that the Punjab was then an ally of France. This is not a part of our textbooks because the Punjab was then ruled by the hated Sikhs. It did not trouble us that at that time our family too was Sikh.

Hamid Pia in turn explained to me how he could cross a busy intersection by ploughing his bike headlong into the fray simply with a loud 'Ya Ali!' And everyone was left aghast, he said. 'Is it a bird? Is it a plane? No, it's Super Panda!' Hamid Pia's sports cycle was a Panda. It was made in China and was grey. I had an Orient. It too was made in China, but was blue.

The advent of bicycles had transformed our lives. He

could get on his bike, plunge through a couple of intersections and appear at my house. I could choose to skip morning assembly, or the last period—using the headmaster's small gate, which was never manned.

His father, Taya-ji Latif, Doctor Rehmatullah's third son, allowed Hamid to only visit my house. But once Hamid Pia reached my house, the city was our oyster. For my father was by then no more.

'Lucky you,' Hamid Pia would jest. He could put a positive spin on any situation.

But that day, dodging the occasional banner screaming, '*Chalo chalo Kabul chalo*', he could not put a positive spin on Juhi Chawla's betrayal. It was unexpected. It was unnecessary. Juhi Chawla's first movie with Amir Khan had taken the Urdu-speaking world by storm. In that movie she had eloped with Amir Khan and they had shacked up in a mountain hideaway until her family had come and killed the couple. Throughout the movie, though, she had maintained a wholesome, girl-next-door image—demure, pure, innocent—an image that we in the land of PTV had never expected from Bollywood. Juhi was different. Juhi was nice.

Until, one day, Hamid Pia had seen on Hall Road the poster of her in steamy hot pants.

Hall Road was the market where all things electronic could be had. VCRs made in Pakistan, tape decks made to order, Walkmans made in Japan, diodes, LEDs, circuit boards, soldering kits, TVs, computers; it was, for a techie, an ever-changing world full of wonder and pleasure. Hamid Pia's school was on Hall Road.

'"Ya Ali" is not correct,' I said.

'"Ya Ali" is not correct?'

'"Ya Ali" is not correct. Nor "*Ya Mohammad**." They told us in school.'

'Someone is working overtime. This I gotta hear!' Hamid was a devout Muslim. He prayed five times a day and wore his religion easily.

'Technically, *ya* in Arabic is meant for people who are present. Hazrat Ali or Hazrat Muhammad are not present,' I explained, 'so you can say Ya Allah but you cannot say Ya Ali or Ya Mohammad.'

'You said it.'

'What?'

'Ya Ali.'

'You cannot say Ya Ali.'

'You said it again.'

'What?'

'Ya Ali.'

'Ya Ali,' I said in mock exasperation.

'So, what you are saying is that now I cannot close my eyes and plunge into an intersection.' Hamid Pia became almost serious.

'I am not saying that. I am just telling you what I was taught. Zayn spent last weekend scratching the "ya" off the stickers on our window. I guess when you are young you believe everything they teach you.'

We were then slowly passing the Hall Road intersection. 'Come, I will show you.' We climbed down and made our

---

*Peace be upon him

way to Vicky Video. I was saddened to see that Hamid Pia was right. Juhi Chawla was indeed wearing hot pants. The only consolation, Hamid Pia muttered, was that she did not appear too happy doing so.

We continued our mission on foot, weaving through baskets of steaming sweet potatoes sunk in coal and pistachios that beckoned to us from their shells, and roasted peanuts and baked corn with lime and chili. With nothing in our pockets, it was easy to avoid these temptations, but even if we had had money we would never eat outside home. That was the way it was. We sauntered homeward with our hands in our pockets.

'Without "Ya Ali" I will be defenceless. Why don't you try crossing Mozang without saying Ya Ali.'

'I am not saying anything. *They* keep coming up with these ideas. I am just telling you.'

'*They* could come up with some ideas on space and relativity. How the speed of light is the only thing that is constant. Maybe there is something about it in the Koran and these guys could come up with a solution to the problem of space travel? Why can't they give us some ideas on that? Why can't they explain everything the way Stephen Hawking explains the universe? Who are these guys and why do they have to keep fixing what is not broken?' Hamid Pia fired away, amused by his questions. He got pleasure in questioning everything. 'So, basically, what they are implying is that I should stop when the light is red.'

'Basically, yes. That would be rational.'

'But belief is not rational,' he responded. 'You think it is rational for me to get up at the crack of dawn to pray?

I get up because I want to. I get up because my Prophet told me to. There is no rationale to this.' He shook his head.

Hamid Pia loved the Prophet the way I loved my father. His voice would break when talking of the Prophet the way mine breaks when I talk of my father.

He did not know who was slowly but relentlessly trying to tell him that his emotions were wrong, his belief deviant.

Hamid Pia was tall. He was also wiry. His mother would fill him up all day but his frame refused to fill out. His mind was the freshest source of rewiring of words, scenarios and situations. He could subtly reword a sentence or reframe a situation and, suddenly, to the initiated, it would become hilarious. He had a sense of place and timing that was almost dangerous. Once, when a bearded guest had just listed the ways in which his five walks to and from the mosque every day had changed his life and his blood pressure, and a solemn group was nodding in appreciation, Hamid Pia had asked plaintively, 'Sir, can't you find God at home?' Everyone had broken into uncontrolled laughter, but Hamid Pia's expression did not change.

He was never cowed by wealth, girth or style. He could hold his own in any situation simply by being himself. No better antidote to swagger than Hamid Pia's stories. Once, as we sat in the midst of a group of boys who were discussing the latest cars, trying to outdo each other in subtle and not subtle hints about their wealth, Hamid Pia could not contain himself. 'We are very rich,' he butted in solemnly. The group conversation stopped. 'In fact we are so rich that we employ a woman solely for the job of opening a tap and then closing it.' The group did not know how to respond to this little bit of information. 'She comes daily, rings the bell, opens the tap in our courtyard and then does nothing else. We give her lunch and then she has a couple of cups of tea with three spoons of sugar and waits until the sun goes down. She then says goodbye, closes the tap and goes home.' The boys did not know what to say. I had to hold my breath because I knew well the cleaning woman he was talking about.

As we walked we found ourselves at the gates of the Hilton. It seemed like a good hotel and we turned in. The lobby was typical Bollywood marble under dim lights, but our noses detected a banquet hall where smartly dressed PTV stars and brightly coloured PTV starlets kept flitting in. We decided to continue our discussion in the back rows of this star-studded affair.

'Islam is quite mathematical. One kalima, five namaz, thirty roza, 2.5 per cent zakat, one hajj. And you are done. Nothing more.' My concepts were clear. I had read all this in Islamiyat and anything that was not mathematical was not Islam for me.

Hamid Pia shook his head for the umpteenth time. 'These are methods. Like torches lighting a path. These are not the path.' Hamid Pia knew that my father had kept me neutral in ways of religion. My father had left it to me and I had left it to my Islamiyat textbooks. 'The path itself cannot be explained, cannot be calculated mathematically. It can only be felt. And feelings cannot be described. Or measured. A full plate of chawal is heaven itself, when you are hungry; a distraction, when you are not. So what then is a plate full of chawal?' he said.

Hamid Pia smirked knowingly and both of us turned to see bearers entering the hall with trays heaped with chawal. End of discussion.

This was the life. We could not stay for tea. We continued up Mall Road. It became green and leafy.

Hamid Pia could understand my schoolbook version of Islam, but I could never fathom Hamid Pia's deep love for the Prophet, for his family, and through them, for Islam. What Hamid Pia could not understand was who kept coming up with newer and newer notions that kept encroaching on his point of view. Who were these people who worked overtime to keep telling Hamid Pia that his feelings were wrong? What we also did not know was that at that very moment Pakistanis were killing each other over these very differences. We were, as it happened, innocently discussing the deepest fault line through political Islam. I would find this out later. Much later.

At that very moment, however, we were faced by a more pressing problem. It seemed there was a second reason we had never eaten anything bazaari until then. We realized too late and almost simultaneously that bazaari food did not agree with us. We both had to go. But where? Instinctively we hailed down a scooter. Hamid Pia got on first. I asked him to get off at the Continental Hotel. 'I will hail down something else and follow.' But the scooter driver would have none of it.

'No, no, no...' he offered eagerly, 'there is more than enough space for three. I insist.' The scooter had a tyre at its back that made it impossible for any passenger to scoot back if needed. This left only half a space between Hamid Pia and the driver. I closed my eyes and squeezed in. Merrily, the scooter took off with Hamid Pia and I spread-eagled like two trophies at the back. Somehow the Continental arrived and we managed to extract ourselves from the scooter. Hamid Pia thanked the scooterwala and the designers of Vespa motorcycles profusely.

We were desperate as we entered the Continental Hotel. 'I hope you know what you are doing.' Hamid Pia was barely audible. The tight-fitting Vespa had bought us some time but not too much.

'This is a hotel. It has hundreds of rooms all attached to washrooms,' I posited. And so we made our way to the elevators and pressed a button at random. When the elevator door opened, it was like in the movies. A hall full of doors. 'Follow me,' I said confidently. We began trying doorknobs undeterred by the fact that all hotels have public washrooms in the lobby. We would find that out later. Much later.

Suddenly a room opened and there was no one inside. 'Allah be praised. Hamid, you go first.'

In a matter of minutes we were done.

But fate had different plans. The bell rang. I had to open the door.

'Housekeeping! Can we make your room, sir?'

'No, no. We are leaving now.'

'Checking out, sir?'

'Yes, yes, checking out the city. We are going now.'

'Should I arrange a car?'

'No, we will walk. We are going on a picnic.'

'Then allow us to pack some food for your picnic, sir.' We needed to escape and I was saddled with the best damned customer service agent I would ever meet in my life.

'We are in a rush, really.'

'No problem, sir, I will call the bakery and you can pick up a box of pastries and patties as you go downstairs, sir.'

'Excellent job, my friend. I will certainly put in a word about your service to your manager.'

We took the elevator to the lobby. Picked up our box and were about to depart when a manager stopped us. 'Should we charge this to your room, sir?' He proffered a folio for signatures. I signed and we ran out of the lobby and stopped only when a kilometre separated us from the gates of the hotel. The gods were smiling on us. We stood with our hands on our knees with a box of bazaari pastries staring us in the face. We could not eat them, we could not take them home and certainly we could not throw them away.

A pathan wearing twenty coats trudged past us the way mountain people trudge—the same way on flat roads as on impossible ridges. We quickly gave him our pastries. 'You must take a coat,' he insisted in return. We could not figure out whether the coats were donating their lice to the man or whether the man was passing on his lice to the coats. We picked up a grey herringbone that somehow fit us both.

Thus in 1987 was born the legend of the 'khandaani' coat. You may have heard fables about it from other children, but what I am to tell you is the true story.

After it was duly washed, we discovered it could be worn with jeans or with a tie. It could be worn when cycling or at a wedding. Hamid Pia would borrow it from me and I would borrow it from Hamid Pia for all the most important occasions: job interviews, college interviews, matchmaking.

The coat travelled between us to at least three continents in the following years. And we accorded it respect. When Hamid Pia met his in-laws for the first time and they asked him why he was not eating much, he explained, to the consternation of his own family and to solemn nods from his future family that he did not want to ruin his khandaani coat. When an air hostess asked if she could take my coat, I would ask her to hang it on a proper hanger for it was khandaani. Children were admonished if they came close to the coat with a plate of chicken biryani, and they would ask their elders the meaning of the word *khandaani*. They argued who would inherit it when Hamid Pia and I passed away. Could a girl inherit the khandaani coat? Could it be passed on while we were still alive?

The khandaani coat made us khandaani too.

Needed, One Passport

> *Life is finite.*
> *Except summers, for the young.*
> —Chachoo Jaidee

In my last summer of school, it was 1988, when my sole aim in life was to somehow complete an entire jog around Race Course Park in Lahore, a series of telephone calls suddenly changed everything.

In a land far far away, a minister finally decided that it was not in his nation's interest to send two high school students to America for the summer. The decision made its way back to America over the phone and a fax was transmitted to American embassies all over the world that two fully paid summer scholarships were now available for high school students—if they could be selected and their travel processed within a week.

The education officer in the American embassy called my principal. My principal called the school's career counsellor. The career counsellor, without hesitation, called the top student in our batch. This boy had consistently been the top grade earner in our school and was perfect in every way. He could go to war to secure marks and he always won those wars. The career counsellor asked him whether he had a passport. He said yes. He was selected.

The principal then called the second boy on his list. This boy was a born genius. We would compete with him to solve equations or square roots and while we frantically solved them on pieces of paper he sauntered to the toilet, did his business, sauntered back to class, and gave us the answer as we struggled to finish. On the road, he could just fall in love with a car's number plate: 'Did you see that one? The first four digits, after the decimal point, of the square root of thirteen?' But that day when the counsellor called, he was not at home. He too had a passport, but he was out of the country.

I was third on the counsellor's list.

I had never received a call from school. Normally, no one did. I recognized the teacher's voice on the other end, so I knew it was not a prank. But I did not have a passport.

'I do not have a passport, sir, but I am sure I can have one made,' I said naively.

'If you can get it by tomorrow, I will be in Pan Am's office on the Mall tomorrow evening,' he said encouragingly.

My next phone call was fateful.

I called Nawaz, my grandfather's driver. I told him that he needed to take me to the passport office in the morning.

Next day, I put on polished black shoes, a clean pair of jeans with a brown belt of my father's and a sky blue polo shirt open at the neck. Going to a government office, like going to war, is fruitless if you are not prepared. Your clothes are your first defence. A government office is not designed for visitors. You will not have drink or food or ventilation. So your clothing must be all cotton. But a cotton shalwar kameez will not help you stand out in the crowd—which you may need to do at times. However, a dress shirt with cufflinks may also be out of place when you have to muscle your way through a door. Polished shoes, for any government servant, are essential. He somehow is unable to believe you if your shoes are not polished—and will ask you to go back in line. The colour of my sky blue shirt was a random choice, but it worked so well that day that I now prefer to wear this colour whenever I need to be sincere with government officers.

I got hold of my birth certificate and any other certificate with my name on it that I could find and arrived at the passport office with Nawaz.

Then Nawaz took over. He knew better than any man I know how the system in any office works. He had also once done a favour for someone who worked in the deep recesses of that office. In the end, I had to appear sincere and needy as Nawaz kept presenting me and my file across a plethora of desks—there always is a procedure to get things done if the office wants it done—and as evening fell my name was called out. I went to the office collection window and my passport, with my name in beautiful handwriting, was hurriedly shoved into my hand. I did not pay a penny in bribe.

We arrived hungry and hot at the Pan Am office, where my counsellor sat haggling at a desk, trying to get seats to Washington, DC, where I would spend the summer, on the Georgetown University campus, in its Rickover science programme.

If I had not got the passport that evening, I would not have got the scholarship and without the scholarship, I would probably not have got into Yale two years later, and all that was because of one unique man, who now drives you to school and who once drove a car into a stadium to the cheers of all those present.

World Cup

CRICKET WORLD CUP
FINAL
Pakistan vs Australia
-WATCH IT LIVE-

BECTON HALL
YALE UNIVERSTIY

A FLIER for the 1992 World Cup was posted outside university dining halls all over northeastern United States; and on the night of the final match, Yale's Becton Hall was teaming with Aussies, Brits, Kiwis, Indians, Lankans, Bengalis, Jamaicans and Pakistanis. Coffee and sandwich stalls were doing solid business. It was midnight and Pakistan was playing England in Sydney.

I was an active member of the cricket club, although tonight, with Pakistan in the finals, I was deep in the centre of a group of other Pakistanis waiting for the auditorium's screen to come alive.

But there was a problem.

As the players took the field, the screen would briefly

tune in and then fade out, repeatedly, as the people manning the screening apparatus kept increasing. My newly formed friends kept asking me to see what was going on. I assured them that we were in good hands, that Yale's Cricket Club had computer scientists and electrical engineers who would be laying the backbone of the world's IT infrastructure for the coming decades, that I would only add to the rush at the controls and accomplish nothing.

They didn't care, they said, they wanted Pakistani eyes on the problem. So I went forward. The satellite dish controller, I was told, kept missing the channel in question, the university's help desk was closed because it was midnight and a weekend, and they had no idea what to tell the crowd of people who had driven so many hours for a glimpse of cricket. The situation was grim.

I rummaged in my pockets and found a quarter.

After I'd found a pay phone and a telephone directory book, I called a sports bar and asked to speak to its owner—Sandy. How I knew Sandy is a story for another day. I explained our predicament. He thought for a while and suggested that maybe the satellite we were aiming for had not been programmed into the dish controller. Thus the channel we wanted showed up only briefly as the dish tracked its path from one pre-programmed satellite to another.

Sandy explained a solution that was breathtaking in its simplicity. Armed with this knowledge, I re-entered the auditorium, which was now agitated beyond reason, and made my way to the front, where I explained briefly what we needed to do. We were by then desperate to try anything.

We restarted the tracking sequence. The crowd moaned as the by-now-familiar sequence of channels tuned in and faded out as the dish, unseen, swivelled along slowly. Then, as the match from Sydney reached its maximum clarity, I signalled another club member and he pulled out the main plug of the multimedia console. The screen went blank. The crowd sighed. Then, with fingers crossed, I asked my friends to turn on everything except the satellite tracking system, in effect jamming it in place.

As the screen came back on, we were suddenly in Sydney. The crowd went wild. Beer bottles cracked open and I was feted all the way back to my chair.

Pakistan won that night in Sydney and that year we also became world champions in hockey and in squash.

It was 1992. And things were looking up.

The World You Inherit

After graduating from Yale in 1994, I decided that I was now old enough. That I had now seen enough books and read enough people to make a reasonable choice when it came to women. I removed from myself, very consciously, the prohibition I had placed against having a girlfriend. The world was now going to be my oyster and the sky was the limit. I left the shores of America on a charter flight to Amsterdam and began making my way via land back to Pakistan. My first target was Istanbul, where I was supposed to meet my friend Sean Flanagan from Yale. We would then go together to Pakistan. I took three weeks to travel from Amsterdam to Paris and then saw Paris like no tourist can.

A brother-in-law of the wife of a cousin of my father had moved to Paris as a factory worker in the 1970s. I called him—mobile phones were not yet found in everyone's pockets—from a phone booth. A young man was then deputed to find me, which he did, and with him I proceeded to the outskirts of the outskirts of the city. We stayed in the shadows for some reason, observing keenly the eyes of each policeman before crossing every road for the police was fierce and they were everywhere. I realized from this prism that I, as a Pakistani, was not a particularly welcome visitor to Paris. Home was in a maze of tall and unforgiving apartment buildings and my relative's family had made a small, cozy remnant of Pakistan on one crevice of one of these buildings. The whole family prayed together and everyone spoke in French. I remember one night, we sat down after ablution and solemn prayer, waiting for dinner, watching the evening news, when the news broke for a commercial. An absolutely naked woman with just a bar of soap held strategically, jumped onto the screen bringing us suddenly into the West. My relative scrambled desperately for the remote but could not find it and the religious serenity of the room was suddenly replaced by an unspeakable unease. The children grew tense and my relative could not change the topic and no one spoke for a long time.

I would leave at five every morning with my relative to a marché where he would sell ladies' fashionwear from the back of a van. He had to buy the right stock every week, he told me, to ensure that he sold what he stocked. He would keep an eye on fashion magazines and on the latest haute couture as catwalk fashion found its way to magazines and then to high-end stores and then to his van. Fashion in Paris changed quickly. It still does, it always has. If he knew what women liked, he could feed his family. He would leave me in charge of the van while he went around looking at what women were buying from other vendors to make sure he knew the trends. A man born in a village close to Rawalpindi, his fingers shaped into blunt iron-working instruments, was today keeping track of fashion on the streets of a hostile Paris. He worked all week. The marché changed every day to a different town and if he did not get up early enough, someone else would park a van in his spot—and on the day off he had to buy stock for the next week according to his judgment of what the trends would favour in the coming days. He had to put food on the table. He had not been home in thirty years and had arrived as a common labourer, without any knowledge of the language, and had worked in factories saving money to bring a wife from home. But it took him too long and now he was old and his children were young and he had to keep going until the children could start work and then he would rest and return home to rest, in his mother's land.

When my stay was coming to an end, I went to the Italian embassy to get a visa.

There, I can still picture it, even before I entered, I could spy through the glass door of the embassy a most flawless of tan complexions, smooth, copper-toned, flashing from between the belt of a jeans and the hem of a snug white top. Making a mental note of this picture, programmed as I was from the days of Chachoo Jaidee and Lahore, I did not go up to her. Instead, I took a form and sat down to fill it. Here the solitary vigil of the Mohicans finally paid off: She came and sat with me and asked me a question on the form, speaking Carribean English. Now I saw her face. She wore very clean glasses and I looked through them straight into her eyes. We both smiled. She was a junior at Princeton. She was going to Nice and so was I. She invited me to join her and her friends to plan the trip to Nice. And here is the regret.

My relative was waiting for me at home with a farewell dinner and a prayer, and so I had to decline the invite.

Cell phones had not yet arrived, remember, and a goodbye meant a goodbye. I would meet her only in another life. And I cannot file that away to God or to chance. It was my decision and I regret it for being the first one, even after my declaration that I would now look for a wife.

I wish I could guide you on this one. I wish I could tell you what decisions you could call me for and which ones you can take on your own. For you can never tell.

You see, there is a time, often in school, before which good boys do not discuss girls. The concept comes under discussion among friends, yes, but only in general, tentative terms. And then, suddenly, as if a collective switch is flipped, the whole group has nothing else to talk about but girls. It is a fantastic time full of possibilities and wonder. Friends become closer, jealousies erupt, dream-filled stories circulate and self-discoveries are made. It is important, before this stage arrives, to know that it will. It is also important, before it does so, to discuss it, not with your friends but with those who have passed through it before you. This is the reason I tell you these stories, so that you are prepared for the eventuality before it sneaks up on you and leaves you breathless.

It is important in such matters to discuss them. If you have a father you can talk to, it is good to discuss them with him. When I was fifteen and my father was months away from his last car ride, we sat in our car with a Coke on Jail Road and discussed girls. He told me that the trouble with girls is that they make friends forget each other. He told me that in the matter of girls it is always best to wait and also to get the right advice (his). He told me that soon all my friends would start talking of girls and they will all start piecing together the mystery of women for the first time. The one-eyed would be leading the blind. It would be crazy and it could be fun but it was important, he told me, never to rush and always to discuss.

The world you inherit will not be the same as mine but women will still be women and boys will still be boys, and the words of my father will still be true for you as they were for me.

Rule Number 1

When I arrived in America in 1990, I realized that the people in the West were so straightforward, so gullible, so believing, that they would not survive a day in Asia. They believed every word I said. With clear eyes, they nodded seriously at my jokes. I had to explain to them 'let's meet for lunch' does not mean that I will be at the dining hall at noon, that 5.30 might mean 5.45 or even 6. 'What a lovely dress!' could mean a hundred things. The art of quickly sifting a sentence for sarcasm—or of steeling oneself for the slowly dawning double entendre—was lost on those shores.

They did not understand.

They could not fathom the neurons we dedicate to constantly filtering all statements, all transactions, for caveats, for weaknesses, for inconsistencies.

When the grocer says the apricots are from Baluchistan, we must pretend to smell and massage the apricots while our brains quickly rummage through old evidence: the Sindhi bananas last month appeared to have come from a cold storage; the sticker on each piece means they were almost good enough to export; you also know where his father lives, and he knows that. This last piece of evidence is the clincher and we then close the deal without really closing the transaction. 'If they are not from Baluchistan, you know I am bringing them back,' you say. The grocer, quickly rummaging through his own mental list of past receivables, starts expertly plonking apricots into your bag, weighing the quality of each piece against the possibility of your actually returning any bad pieces, your expertise in spotting a bad piece at the bottom of the bag, and of course the percentage of his own bad inventory that he must pass on to each customer on average.

This transaction does not take place in silence. The gaps are filled with remonstrations, jibes, promises and reminders of the Almighty's power to blacken the tongue of the untruthful—which we all know are just polite fillers, social graces, not to be taken literally. Now, how can the Western mind possibly learn all this when even we need constant practice? If we go abroad for a few years, we too begin to trust.

Take Asim Ejaz, one of the brightest minds Pakistan has produced. He was my junior in school, got a perfect score in his SATs, and went on to become a professor of economics at Harvard. One summer, he came back to Pakistan on sabbatical to visit his father. The father, happy to have him home, sent him to buy a cartload of bricks. When the bricks arrived, the father realized to his horror, that the bricks were baked with salty mud. He could not believe his son could make such a simple mistake. His son could not believe that he was expected to be an expert on the production process of bricks. But the father was not appalled at his son's lack of knowledge in the fine art of making bricks. He was shocked that his son had forgotten the fundamental building block of our society: never to trust a man selling bricks.

If you sign a letter of intent, remember that it does not mean anything if money has not changed hands. If you sign an agreement, read it again and again for the hook. A hook is an innocuous-sounding, goodwill-inducing statement that could, if taken literally, allow a signing party to just walk away. I have seen many such written hooks in my time but the most often used, spoken one, is 'inshallah'—spoken at the end of a promise, generally used after setting a meeting time, but sometimes at the end of any solemn handshake. I too use it often, thereby retaining the right to call myself a Pakistani.

You can now understand why, on instinct, without having to really debate the issue, I was able to discover, in my late teens, a credo by which I have been able to conduct myself ably through life on the morally windswept shores of the East. I call this credo Rule Number 1.

Rule Number 1: Do Not Trust Anyone East of the Hindu Kush.

When I share this credo here in the land of the pure, people nod seriously, cringe for a moment at its unambiguous sweep, but generally accept its validity in the final analysis. People on distant shores find such generalizations appalling and almost never agree. Trust is one of the tenets of their society. As I have said, even I tend to forget Rule Number 1 after six months in the West.

I remember when I arrived in Pakistan in 1994 after college, having travelled by road through much of Europe, Central Asia and China. My friend Sean Flanagan and I entered through Gilgit and made our first stop in Pakistan in Abbottabad, in the empty house of an aunt of a friend where we could shower and eat. We then walked around the town, relaxed, full, and finally in Pakistan. As we sat on a leafy park-bench, we were approached by a red-cheeked young man with barely a bristle on his chin. He explained to us his problem, that he had arrived from Chilas to visit his mother in hospital, but his mother had already been discharged. Now he needed money to go back to Chilas. We had very little money of our own but were now not far from Lahore, so I gave him enough for bus fare and a meal. After he left, Sean asked me to translate the conversation. Upon listening it, he quickly brought up Rule Number 1. I laughed and said, 'No, no...the Rule is too general: one must use one's own judgment.' I explained that this was my own country and I could better read the lay of the land. I stressed that he should definitely follow the Rule as a foreigner, but I, hailing from this land, could judge and decide from case to case. I had just negotiated my way through twenty countries—without visas for two of them—through two civil wars, through drug dealers and the Red Army. I could deal with a kid from Chilas.

My words fell on deaf ears. Sean Flanagan was already jogging towards the park exit.

Without really exchanging words, like two practised hunters, we began fanning out, keeping each other in sight, signalling deftly to quickly track the boy down. We saw him talking to some men on the other side of the street, but before we could get to him, he began moving purposefully towards the city centre. We followed at a distance and on opposite sides of the street. The kid picked up pace but did not look back. Soon he arrived at the main bus stand. We waited around a corner as he negotiated with a bus driver. We saw him change money and then get onto the bus as the driver stood by waiting for it to fill up.

My judgment was proven correct. The Rule stood broken by a young man from Chilas.

But something was just not right.

I asked Sean Flanagan to go back and wait for me in the park, and I made my way through parked buses getting cleaned. From a side where I could not be seen, I got into another bus getting serviced. I could now clearly see the young man sitting in the bus—alone. He could not see me. I waited for a good few minutes. The boy then got up, got his money from the bus driver, looked around and started walking out of the bus station. I called out to him and he began to run. I did not follow.

I walked back to the park and told Sean Flanagan that he was right. Rule Number 1 was still valid. Only, I was out of touch.

So, when in doubt, stick to Rule Number 1.

OutSource

The idea for OutSource had first come to me when I was in college in the US. I lay in a hospital bed, recovering from surgery for an old injury I had received on a road on the way to Gojra with my father. In the hospital I had seen my doctor speaking into a little recording device. The cassette that had held his voice would then be sent to an agency where trained medical transcriptionists would transcribe his words into written medical records. Could we send this voice to Pakistan? Could we get it transcribed there instead? That idea continued to fascinate me as I finished my degree and slowly made my way back to Pakistan.

The Internet was then still young. Microsoft Word would put a red squiggle under the word *internet*. Internet was not yet a part of Microsoft's dictionary. But it had arrived in Pakistan.

This Internet, available through cumbersome phone modems, was normally slow, but I discovered that if you were willing to stay up late at night, the entire bandwidth could be yours to download large voice files.

Once this voice arrived in Pakistan, it could be transcribed at a fraction of the cost, overnight, and be delivered with an email back to the hospital it came from.

I could not wait to put my idea to work because I would not be the only person to have got it. I called it OutSource Inc.

I explained my business plan to my friend Ali Hyder and brought him into it. I developed a logo, a brochure, an office and a team of doctors trained to transcribe, and then I returned once again to the US to try to sell the idea, to get our first order.

Getting that first order was tougher than anything I have had to do. A team of transcriptionists sat in Pakistan with salaries ticking like a bomb. Each day in the US cost real dollars. Each meal was in hard currency. Each phone call cost money. I had to have a cell phone so I could respond to any eager client and also a way to respond to emails on the road. I borrowed my cousin's Acura and a map of the United States.

Every county in every US state has a free public library with free Internet access and washrooms. These county libraries became my office on the go. I would park the Acura on a highway truck stop and go to sleep in the back—turning on the heater at night in small bouts when the cold got really unbearable. This became my home. I would shave and wash in the truck stop and be ready for business every morning.

I had a list of possible clients: transcription companies and clinics all over the eastern United States, whom I would call, make appointments with and visit, one by one, with the khandaani coat and a tie and a brochure and a visiting card.

Perseverance and doggedness, are the two real rules of marketing. A salesman can never give up. He thrives on hope and the promise of every new day, of every new bend in the road. But even the best of salesmen have a breaking point.

God knows I was close to mine when, having travelled all the way from New York to the tip of Florida, I was back in Washington, DC, only a few hours away from the place where I had started from—New York City—when I finally met a man who was willing to take a chance on us.

Jay Jaiswal was an Indian Punjabi businessman who ran his own transcription company. His fingers were covered in gemstone rings and his office was the sleekest I had ever seen. He did not take long to size me up.

'I will give you a test run tonight. If you guys pass, you have my business,' he said. And that was that. We exchanged FTP site addresses and text templates, and then discussed his passion for cars and for Lahore. I called up Ali Hyder and the team of doctors in Lahore as I came out. Tonight was going to be the night. I had given the details to my team, my work was done for the evening.

The team would now have to do what they had been training for. They would have to download the voice files to a server, distribute them to all team members, transcribe the sessions into the format provided, proofread and upload the document files back to the server before Jay Jaiswal's office opened the next morning in the suburbs of Washington, DC. All I could do was pray to the gods of load shedding and bandwidth—nothing more.

I had by then returned the Acura to my cousin in North Carolina and was on my way back to New York. My luggage was stored in a locker in a bus stop. I went back to it, carefully put the khandaani coat on a hanger, put on jeans and a sweatshirt, and began roaming through the city of Washington. My job here was done. If we were not successful, I would not have the cash to travel anywhere other than to JFK International Airport in New York. Tonight would simply have to be the night. I found a stone bench on Washington's grassy National Mall near a monument. I washed my face in a drinking fountain and on that stone bench I prayed with tears in my eyes. I talked to God, one-on-one, with no one in between. Not for the last time in my life, I had reached the end of all my resources and so I prayed. And then, somehow, I knew—that I would get the order in the morning. It was simple then. I snuggled into a newspaper on that bench and went to sleep while my team toiled more than seven thousand miles away, on the other side of the globe.

When morning arrived and I got to Jay Jaiswal's office, the team in Lahore had shipped everything back in time and on cue. I put my game face on and negotiated a price and a contract on two simple pieces of paper. I shook hands and we were in business. It was that simple.

∞

Two simple pieces of paper. I have, for many years now, been perplexed by the importance of those two sheets of paper, which were all the security Jay Jaiswal needed to trust me, a man from another continent, not just from another city.

For that is not how we do business in Pakistan. When we do business, hire an employee or even choose a doctor, we investigate. We find out about the person's village, his father and about his friends. We double check and triple check; because we exist in a space with very little rule of law.

Rule of law. Remember these three words. They are the difference between the developed and the developing.

Rule of law allowed Jay Jaiswal to trust a total stranger with no background in business to start a new global operation. I cannot create rule of law but rule of law can create many small businessmen like me.

Confidence

With OutSource launched, I thought I could marry any woman in the world. I was poor and unknown, but I had started my own company and sold a new idea to strangers in distant lands and was paying salaries, and I thought now I could do anything I wanted to.

Onto this very confident stage came Wajiha, or Woodge. Woodge's family and our's had known each other for four generations. Our humour and our roots were quite similar. Because of this, with exquisite decorum, both parties had been trying, since two generations at least, for a *rishta* between them. But every time something happened.

It was, therefore, decided by the respective parties that Woodge and I would be introduced with blessings from both families and allowed to decide for ourselves. Woodge's parents had emigrated to Australia and she had come to Pakistan only a few times in her life. She did not speak Urdu and did not know what was in store for her when she came to Lahore and I came to pick her up from her grandmother's home. She answered the bell herself and I opened the door to my third-hand red Suzuki FX 800. Before I could take the car away from the house, she had explained to me that she had no intentions of moving to Pakistan or of getting married. Immediately, I too piped in my intentions of never moving to Australia and quickly poured scorn on the very idea of marriage. We quickly agreed that we were not made for each other and that I would tell her parents. A smell of gloom and excitement, and hormones, permeated the air as I revved the reluctant FX past 40 kilometres per hour.

We knew what we were not going to do. But we still had a week to kill before telling her parents.

So I took her to our home one day, and on the next to a cheap Urdu cinema, where they had to put chairs in the aisle to fit us in and where in the middle of the movie a woman lost her ticket and Woodge, to the astonishment of everyone including myself, quickly took out her cigarette lighter and found it. On the following day I took her to the local Salt & Pepper, where my cousin Aamir Bhai—the second son of the second son of my grandfather, Doctor Rehmatullah—saw us, but diplomatically kept the sighting to himself. We had in fact the best fun, that a boy and a girl can have in Lahore, Woodge and I. Zero guilt, zero fear, and best of all, zero expectations; I got a slice of Australian freedom right here in Lahore. The families would have to wait another decade before trying for a rishta again. I think this method of matchmaking will likely still be in force when you are old enough to have your own FX. Remember, in that case, to shake the girl's hand when you meet her and shake it again when you say goodbye—or the sanction will be no more.

Robbery

About this time, a few years into OutSource, sometime in the late 1990s, a man came to the dentist's clinic across the hall from our office in Lahore. Here, while chatting to the dentist, he could see the array of PCs lining our walls and discovered that OutSource was closed on weekends. So, over the weekend, he organized a raiding party and stole all our computers.

We should not have survived, but we did. A case was filed in the local police station. A month later, the thieves fell out over a gambling debt and were ratted out by one of their own. The police began investigating and the thieves began confessing. It seemed they were running a lucrative trade in robbing offices and selling PCs, and I was going to get a crash course in how the law worked.

It worked pretty well for the most part. Pretty soon, all my PCs were located. Half had been sold to a shop in Hafeez Centre. They were easily recovered and the shop even sent a repairman to the police station who was already busy assembling the units in the office of the personal assistant of the superintendent of police when I arrived. Neither the shopkeeper nor the repairman was under any kind of stress as they quietly went about re-assembling the PCs. In fact,

I was obliged to tip the repairman to ensure that he did a serviceable job, and in time became good enough friends with him that he asked that I use his services for future business in Hafeez Centre. He told me that he and the shopkeeper were members of the Sipah-e-Sahaba, a jihadi militia funded by the military for jihad in Kashmir but based in the south of Punjab. He told me that the jihadi organization was his 'backing' and that that was why he had joined. The police could therefore take the PCs but knew they could not arrest him. Both coexisted comfortably with each other. The only two parties uncomfortable in this transaction were me and the culprits who had done the actual stealing without a backing of their own.

The poor bastards who stole my computers, twelve years after that robbery, are still in prison, awaiting trial.

I could not recover the other half of my stolen PCs, even though I knew where they were.

This is what happens when there is no rule of law. Everyone then gathers around tribes, or mafias, or unions, or religious parties, to have their own backing to then negotiate from positions of strength, where justice is yet another negotiation.

The remaining half of my stolen PCs had been sold at Hall Road. The Police Superintendent told me that he could not help me there. He could tell me the name of the shop where my PCs were sold and that the PCs were still there, but he could not help me recover them because the Hall Road Traders Union was very powerful and their backing was stronger than him.

The man who was telling me this was six-feet tall and

ruggedly good looking, if battered by time. His desk did not have any paper or pen and his hands were built like spades for digging. He was very polite to me and explained that if I had any way of approaching the Hall Road Traders Union, I was free to try. This man himself had a very strong backing.

Back in the time of General Zia, he had been the SHO—station house officer—of Liberty Market Police Station when the country's most famous movie star was gang-raped by assailants who entered her house near Liberty Market. When newspapers carried the story, General Zia announced that he would find the culprits at all costs. A mega police dragnet did find them and all confessed. One of the culprits was the then SHO of the police station of Liberty Market. He now sat in front of me. He and all the other suspects had eventually escaped punishment in mysterious circumstances when the movie star's only son was suddenly kidnapped and she withdrew her case and emigrated to Bangladesh instead—despite General Zia.

This scary man was telling me that the Hall Road Union had a backing that was stronger than him.

I had to check this out. I wanted my PCs back. So I went to the shopkeeper who promptly referred me to the union president and I quickly got to the point. I asked him who his backing was. He laughed. He said he was backed by the biggest back there was. I laughed back.

All unions are in the end democratic entities and would eventually be backed by one of the two major political parties. So I asked him which political party he was aligned to. 'The army,' he said. I asked him to be serious. I told him that I was a businessman like him and wanted to make a deal. I did not want bullshit, I wanted the facts. He was nonplussed. He said he was serious. 'Go to the GOC 10 Div,' he said, 'you will get your confirmation, but even he will not be able to get you your computers.'

I was not going to give up that easily. One of my relatives had retired as a senior general. I went to him and explained the curious case of the union leader who said he was the army's man. My uncle laughed on hearing me say this, but he was senior enough to pick up the phone and talk to the general commanding the 10 Div. He did not laugh when he put the phone down. It seemed there was some truth in what the union president was claiming.

On coming to power, Musharraf had imposed a sales tax against which the traders had protested. To finish these protests, the army had struck a deal with most of the large market unions. They would not collect sales tax from them, but the union office holders would be appointed by the army. So, yes, the man was correct. He was from the army party and, yes, his backing was the army.

I then went to meet the GOC, 10 Div, as well. He too was very polite. He asked me to write an application.

I never got those computers back from Hall Road. But I did learn a lesson on rule of law.

That lesson, and the guilt of a wrong yet to be put right, forced me again and again to street corners, when an unlikely chief justice with a moustache, in a strange twist of fate, decided to challenge Musharraf in order to save his own job.

Caught between the devil and the deep blue sea, we chose the devil. It did not matter to us that the chief justice with the moustache had himself validated Musharraf's martial law. It did not matter to us that we had turned what was the chief justice's battle to save his job into our battle for the rule of law. I will tell you later. It did not matter to us that we were readying the grounds for a possible dictatorship by an unchecked judiciary in the years to come. It did not matter.

We needed a hero.

Ninety-Seven Days

When OutSource was doing well, I could not get girls to marry me. It was impossible to explain to potential fathers-in-law exactly what it was that I did. They came over with vague ideas of what a Yalie was supposed to be, and left bemused and confused at what I was trying to do.

'So, what exactly do you sell?' they would eventually ask.

After countless proposals thus withered away, my special bond with God got stronger. The careless banter my family has with God became a serious discussion, at the end of which I told Him that He could worry about the matchmaking business while I concentrated on OutSource. I told Him that I would say yes to any rishta and that He better be careful what He threw my way, for now, the Divine was fully in charge. I would not say no, I told Him.

It was in this state of mind that the rishta of a girl who wore a hijab came through the door. And I was not going to say no. That was my deal with God. Her father, a very liberal man, surprisingly approved me for the second round. Then Zara, her husband, Sheri Bhai, and I went to call on them, and after a few pleasantries, I was left alone with the girl and her sister.

The sister's first question to me was on the role of women in Islam.

I could see their lawn from the window and a gate at the far end and a chowkidar manning the gate and a clear road outside. I thought of Maaji. I thought about large fields of cotton and of the prickly stubble that singed her fingertips as she picked each flower of its soft white down. And I began my answer; philosophical, and correct. And thus it progressed. The two girls asked biblical questions and I answered with the truth. They asked me how many times I prayed in a day. I was, at that time, in the most religious phase of my life and was very glad this question was asked and replied truthfully that I prayed 3.5 times a day. It was a surprise that this was a surprise for them. They asked again and I explained that on some days I went for all five but on others I barely managed one or two. And thus it went from Moses to Abraham to Joseph with my knowledge of the scriptures stretched to its limits. We talked thus of Big Things until they finally asked me whether I had any questions of my own.

I said in all truthfulness that I did not have any questions but did have a suggestion.

Without a hint of sarcasm—for I was absolutely serious—I told them that life does not run on Big Things. If they wanted to choose a life partner they should ask him about the small things in life, the kind of things that help in choosing a fellow traveller or a teammate. A journey would be far easier if one could understand the partner's jokes or if a partner offered to carry the other's bags for a while. On a journey, Big Things like religious persuasion would stay in the trunk of the car.

Both nodded in earnest. I thought I made sense and I also thought my deal with God was now working. If it was hijab He wanted, then hijab it was going to be.

With that I asked the girl whether she had arrived at a decision. She said that she would pray and get guidance from God and would let me know. I asked how soon she expected the guidance from God to arrive and she said she would ask the question after the asr prayer and maybe by maghrib she would know for sure.

She then asked me what my decision was. I replied that her answer would also be my answer. I added that the only difference between me and her was that she was going to ask God and that I had already told Him.

Then we all came home to wait for the word from God to arrive.

The phone did not ring after asr and it did not ring till maghrib and then a whole day passed and the phone still did not ring. God was testing my nerves. Muezzins called the faithful to prayer five times a day. Chachoo Jaidee and I ate kinnoos in front of a gas fire every night and Ali Hyder inquired every morning, but no word came down. Diplomats came and went but to no avail and then, a week later, her parents came to visit. By this time, it was a philosopher and a poet, not a mechanical engineer, who received them.

After tea and samosa, I sat down with the father, dignified and graceful in his repose but helpless in front of faith. And I asked him about the word from God. I told him about the expectations of a maghrib deadline but he stayed quiet instead. As his silent answer hung pregnant in the air, I had to decide not only how to interpret the silence but also how to respond to it.

So, slowly, I told him a long long story from the heart.

There was once a lowly soldier who fell for the beautiful daughter of a very rich merchant. The girl said that she would marry him if he stood below her window every night for one hundred nights and so the soldier took a small stool and a coat and stood below her window. He stood for ten days and then for ten more. He stood while people made fun of him and he stood when dogs urinated on him and he stood when garbage men threw trash on him. He stood for fifty days and every night the girl would open her window and find him standing in the cold. She would then close her window. She opened her window after ninety days and he was still there and she opened it again after ninety-seven days. Hungry and dirty and forsaken, he was still there. Then, with only two more nights to go, as she closed the window the ninety-seventh time, the soldier suddenly got up, took off his coat, picked up his stool, and went home. Never to return.

If she could not pity him after ninety-seven days, she would not be able to love him after a hundred.

The father, a gentleman, nodded slowly, and that was that.

God, I think, had the final word.

God and love are a dangerous mix left to their own. But it was not always this way. I was always afraid of love and I always looked God in the eye. And thus the two often stayed on separate planes.

Love and God

I NEVER got a handle on either Love or God without my father. It was not that they did not exist. They did exist. I knew this because I felt them both in my chest more than once. Love will find you again and again, and each time it will be different and lovely and sad. And God is a part of you that you will lose slowly, seeping out of your skin as you age, replaced either by wisdom to see the truth that cannot be told—only felt—or by regret for seeing God seep out through your fingers.

But first to love, which you would already have felt—for faces in the crowd that would just make your day. It hits early on and crushes you in an embrace again and again.

My first crush was on a girl who used to sing with my sister in a TV programme for children. I was ten. She was of course much older than me, but I was old enough to know how lovely she was. Television was then moving from black and white to colour and the stock children's show was a programme of songs where every week a few new songs were presented by a large chorus of children sitting on three terraced levels in a studio. Me, my sister and a bunch of my cousins would go every week to record because Chachoo Khalid, the sixth son of Doctor Rehmatullah, was a TV director. I would get to sit in the terraced wooden benches and swing on cue with fifty other children while recorded music was played in the background. The sound recordings carried voices of only three good singers. One of them was my sister and another a girl whose name I never knew but whose face, I still remember, was almost Chinese in that she had large sleepy eyes and a small nose and always gave me the impression that she was very bravely facing the world against almost heroic obstacles and I would always want to help her in her stoic stance with an uncoiling inside me that occurred whenever again I felt that pure twinge of love.

I felt it for the last time, Hyder, when I saw your mother walking towards me on our wedding day, when she looked so beautiful that I could not steady my gaze on her and I knew there was a God, and I was at peace with Him and myself. This was the autumn of 2001, in October. At long last, a gaping hole had been filled and I was whole and my internal conversation with God was laid to rest. But then, if you are the groom and also the chief organizer at a wedding, romance always has to compete for every inch of space in your heart. As I kept my long-restrained but now pounding heart in my chest, I also had to keep an eye out for the head of my family, Taya-ji Hafeez, the eldest son of Doctor Rehmatullah, who was late. I had arrived without him. I had to keep an eye on the clock because we had to ride five hours to Lahore and then feed everyone at our house and then make sure they had a place to sleep. I had to make sure Aamir Bhai got a ride to the bus stop and to find a rapprochement between the two families who were suddenly not speaking to one another. I did not want to take any calls from the office because OutSource was running aground, churning out transcripts as our clients cancelled contracts, frightened of war because the invasion in Afghanistan had begun a hundred miles from where I stood. Your mother's cousins had demanded more money than I could give and I had to bargain them down viciously and arrogantly at the same time—not for the last time in my life. And I would lose all balance every time I looked at your mother, soft, serene and smiling. And all would be well.

Our car was not garlanded because daisy cutter bombs were falling in Jalalabad. We moved out as evening began to fall. Sheri Bhai drove and Zara put in a magical CD and I held your mother's soft hand for the first time and held it all the way to Lahore. I stared at her face for four hours unabashed and unashamed and Sheri's car lost the rest on the road. We rode in the privacy of the night, an unreal journey with a full October moon washed and clean, hanging from the window. Unadulterated love seeped from my fingers and your mother's hands were softer than anything I had ever imagined. Having searched for love in flowers and fragrances and embassies and in colleges and dances and springs, I found it within me instead—in the moment, to be felt, to be enjoyed, to be trusted, not to be explained or expressed or analysed. Much like God.

My father's sister, Phuppo Shehnaz, received us when we got home in the night and she oiled the hinges of the verandah door and though my father was not there, his sisters and brothers and their children were all there as much as he would have been. I felt at home in my home just as my father did when he had brought his bride to the home of his father. I wish that you too can bring your bride to such a full household and feel the leaves change colour as you relax in the company of your own. Then I paid my cousins, still more money, to get into my bedroom—each rupee pounding the depths of my fast-emptying pockets.

And then God arrived in a place where of all places I believed he had no business. Not that I have anything against God, but there is a time and a place for everything.

Teeming with advice, Ali Hyder produced a pamphlet he said was his religious duty to give me and which I should read as a guide to marital bliss in the light of Quran and Sunnah as proposed by 'correct' Islamic scholars. I was now told to read through the pamphlet so that he could be assured that he had done his duty by me. I had known Ali Hyder long enough to tell him that I shall gladly take the pamphlet but would not read it. Remember, last-minute advice will come from many quarters when you get married. Never listen to it. Never. Even if the advice is coming supposedly from God. This is not the time for second guesses.

Unfortunately for me, I forgot to tell your mother this. She read the pamphlet from God from cover to cover like a good girl. I had to pay for that, for many years, after that. Such was the import of that pamphlet, that it took on the form of a second mother-in-law, who lived right in our bedroom until, after much coaxing and exercise, over many years, I was able to banish its remains from the vestiges of your mother's innocent mind. I learnt, not for the first time in my life, that God, in His religious form, should be allowed into the home only with a chaperone.

Then I understood why, decades ago, my grandfather,

a very devout man for his day, forbade one of my chachis from attending religious congregations for women—without giving any reason. He just forbade her and as in those days, men did not have to stoop to explanation, the grounds for this historic decision were hotly debated but scrupulously followed for a couple of decades after that with the simple explanation that we do not do that sort of thing. That was fine. But now I know. I never read the pamphlet that had such a long-term impact on my marital bliss but the word of God is so powerful, I now know, that even an outside reference of His leanings for or against a concept, can kill it or sanctify it in the blink of an eye.

I do not say that God does not exist. I am just saying, be careful of what you hear on the street.

IV
WAR BY ANY OTHER NAME

Invasion

GEORGE W. Bush says he looked deep into the eyes of Musharraf and knew instinctively that he could trust him. This was a clear violation of Rule Number 1. And we paid for it.

The Taliban, on the other hand, like the true believers that they are, stuck religiously to Rule Number 1. We paid for that as well.

∽

Days after 9/11, the head of our intelligence service met Mullah Omar, the head of the Taliban, in Kandahar. His assignment was to convince the Taliban to give up Osama and be spared an invasion. This meeting was a major turning point and there are a lot of stories about it. Some say our man double-crossed the Americans and told the Taliban to stand their ground. Others say the Americans too were complicit and wanted to have the satisfaction of invading a foreign country.

However, if one assumes that the Taliban, experienced practitioners of the Eastern arts, were well acquainted with Rule Number 1, the meeting was useless to begin with. There was no way that the Taliban were going to believe us—and vice versa. It does not matter what was said or not said at the meeting. Neither party had any way of solemnizing their point of view with hard collateral. Therefore, there was nothing substantial to believe. Osama was not handed over. The country was invaded.

Since that day, the Afghan Taliban have enjoyed a privileged position, as well as the pasture land of our tribesmen, but even then they do not trust us. They believe we are American stooges and that we will stab them in the back at the first instance. We, in return, do not trust them and do not appreciate their talking directly to the Americans or to the Qataris or to the Turks without us.

Thus it was that the Taliban leadership, under our strict watch, settled in Quetta and in Karachi, while their minions populated the tribal badlands called FATA*. In FATA, the economy remembered the heady days of the last war. Jeep rentals increased. Mountain shacks went up in price. Houses were bought in hard foreign cash. If you held any sort of capital in FATA, you were getting richer but your neighbours kept getting weirder and weirder.

These new neighbours, apart from hard cash and guns, also had the status of holy warriors. That made it easier to give one's daughter away to these marauders in order to survive in this new war economy. In a few years, the motley crew settled down. They had never really had it so good. In comparison to the war-wrecked desert hills of Kandahar, the fertile valleys of our country were ripe and

---

*Federally Administered Tribal Areas

lush and peaceful. In comparison to the ruthless warlords of Afghanistan, the doddering tribal chiefs who ruled these belts were paper tigers. These Pakistani tribal chiefs were also as unpopular as any incumbent is after forty years. Very soon, these softies, so long on the payroll of our government, began getting assassinated. Two hundred died in two years. Anyone who could now claim to be a tribal chief made sure he never entered the tribal area. The motley crew had always had a sanction from God and from the Pakistan Army, but now they did not need anyone's sanction. They were independent.

The first four years of the invasion were placid. Beards were shaved. An Arab was captured hiding in a safe house in Pakistan every other month. A tribal chief was assassinated by unknown assailants once a week. Maulvis protested twice a year. Opium crops flourished in Afghanistan. Property prices boomed in Peshawar. A lot of delegations came and went. Life settled into a smooth routine.

So smooth that just to keep things lively Bush invaded another country.

Things then began to unravel.

The few Pakistanis who still believed that the war on terror was in fact a war against terrorists now had to accept the theory that it was indeed a war against Islam. Rule Number 1 expanded its sweep to include Americans as well.

At the same time, the Taliban, seeing that the Americans had taken their eye off the ball, began installing shadow governors in Afghan provinces, stepping up resistance and hitting Americans with IEDs and suicide bombs.

This upset the entire apple cart. And things began to fall apart.

∽

Who was in charge of the Taliban? We were.

Why were they disturbing the apple cart? Because they came with us up to the escape and sanctuary part but were not really on board with the sitting and waiting part. Rule Number 1 was pasted outside Mullah Omar's door.

Fingers were pointed. Bodies of young men began arriving in Carolina and Texas, and also in Cardiff and Dusseldorf and Milan. Suddenly all eyes were on FATA.

Reluctantly, troop reinforcements were sent into FATA, and London and Berlin and Washington were satisfied.

But all was not well in FATA.

My cousin Zayn, who could kill a buffalo with a bread knife, was a major when he arrived with his troop reinforcements in FATA to appease the accusing fingers of Washington and Berlin and Rome and London. He saw with deep-furrowed consternation men younger than him, dashing and buccaneer, holding vast swathes of land in absolute control. Shops closed and entire villages would leave their homes to welcome young men in Toyota 4x4s, sporting gun belts and beards. These young brigands were fully invested in war. Were it not for war, they would be grinding out lives as bus conductors and jeep drivers. But war allowed them to rule an area larger than Belgium. They had divided it up among themselves, taxed it and ruled it.

Zayn moved his troops in as all armies have moved

troops in for millennia. Slowly, and in the plain view of all brave enough to witness such a sight. He made camps and sentry posts and road checkpoints. And then he settled in. The 4x4s too scattered around and waited.

And everyone else waited as well.

But nothing happened.

Zayn was not ordered to wrestle land back from these Toyota hordes. He had been mobilized only because fingers were being pointed in Washington and in London. Rule Number 1, though, did not allow our generals to trust the fingers in Washington and London. They thought this was a ploy, a ruse by the great powers to move Pakistan's regiments away from the Indian border. Our generals were not going to fall for such a ploy. They had a ruse of their own up their sleeves. They sent only skeleton formations into FATA, not really moving in with full force but creating the impression of a large movement. To create an impact larger than their footprint, these troops were instructed to simply unleash fire into the night.

Zayn was not sent to rescue the population from these 4x4 occupiers. He was here only to be seen to be here.

Thus, Zayn's skeleton troops and these suddenly cavalier marauders began to slowly inhabit the same space, both settling in for a few years of nervous coexistence. The routines of each side were puzzling for any local man who had to travel these parts. He would be stopped, frisked, and checked for papers and guns by Zayn's fixed army picket. After a thorough check, he would be allowed to carry on. A kilometre's travel would bring him to a 4x4 picket. The same would happen there again.

Then, at night, Zayn's skeleton formation would fire artillery into the night with a lot of noise and clamour. For the locals, this was very disconcerting. They would hear heavy gunfire all through the night; and then, in the morning, the same pickets would still be standing guard on the same spots, unscathed.

Musharraf's army did not interfere with local affairs. They thought they were allowing the locals to handle their affairs through age-old customs. But, in fact, they were allowing the marauders to gain control over the population under the very noses of the army. The marauders now decided property disputes. They had their choice of women to marry. They began distorting age-old customs to suit their whims. A majority of honest local men had to leave their women and children to work in far off places. These women and children were now under the control of the nouveau powerful gangsters.

Yet public opinion in the plains of Punjab and in the urban clamour of Karachi persisted against any military operation against these elements. Rule Number 1 made sure that people like me, who insisted the 4x4 marauders were an occupying army within Pakistan were continually dismissed as propagandists.

Then, as a final nail in the coffin of the local population, massive aid began arriving from the United States; development schemes would wean these people away from their terror-mongering ways. The US Congress earmarked $1.1 billion and disbursed it over nine years, through the FATA secretariat, to local contractors for road works, water channels and school buildings. Nothing was built but the funds were disbursed. Funds to local contractors were easily extorted by the most powerful of the marauders. With these funds, the petty marauders became warlords—more powerful than the skeleton army units sent in to police them.

Everyone who watched this transformation from ragtag marauders to bona fide warlords began to wonder how shoe-polish boys could possibly amass such power.

Zayn's boss—who worried about paying college fees for his children and who had to work with overhauled, ten-year-old jeeps—could not understand how new 4x4s kept making their way to unkempt brats who had no brigadier to answer to, no annual confidential report to worry about and a growing reputation among the population. It was natural for him to suspect a foreign hand. How else could it be possible. A conspiracy against the motherland was what it was. We could not trust anybody. Anyone could be a spy working for the enemies. Anyone could be an enemy. Rule Number 1 went into overdrive.

༄

'The Americans have planned out everything. Everything. Ever since we went nuclear, the Americans had a plan. They will degrade us until we give them the bomb.'

Chachoo Jaidee had switched from Rothman's to Gold Leaf. His forehead had become broader and with Chachi he now had three strapping boys. He peeled the plastic off the little red box in a practised circle, crinkled the wrapping and took a customary whiff as the gold wrapper first parted to reveal a row of sweet-smelling tobacco.

'It is all a part of America's plan,' he said.

Zayn was back home from the war and we huddled together on Chachoo Jaidee's car engine. Zayn too smoked as all officers do. But he could not smoke in front of Chachoo Jaidee. He laughed his laugh that rocked the neighbourhood. 'It is more complicated, Chachoo.' A small tray of tea mugs balanced precariously between the battery and the air filter. Sweat rolled down my hand as I picked up a cup, silently.

'Look at the corruption. Look at our leaders. We are not as bad as all this. You know it. This is all planned.' Chachoo pointed to a window behind him. He had to, only last month, change all his window panes. All of them had suddenly exploded one day as he was nursing his morning tea. All of them. In the bedrooms, in the living room, in the bathroom, all of them had smashed with a huge bang. 'The good thing about a shock wave,' Chachoo explained, 'is that it creates low pressure outside the house. So all the windows explode outwards. If they had exploded inwards, I would have had it.' Chachoo still had a knack for explaining things.

I was silent, not rocking the boat. Zayn laughed, rocking the neighbourhood again. 'The bomb that broke your windows was not planted by the Americans, Chachoo. It was planted by the Taliban.'

'We do not know that.' Chachoo replied. 'I know you do not agree but we do not know that.' Chachoo grabbed a screwdriver and revved the throttle.

While we debated, the Rightly Guided Taliban of Afghanistan kept parcelling out pieces of Pakistan to these marauders. Through a webcast a warlord could be anointed an emir—a warlord of warlords.

These warlords called themselves Taliban. This word had its own currency in those times. It was good to be Taliban. People respected you if you were Taliban. Men from Karachi to Lahore wished that they too could be Taliban. Taliban, for many Pakistani men, were the culmination of 1,400 years of struggle to achieve again the purity of that golden period of the Rightly Guided Caliphs that we had all been taught in our Islamiyat textbooks.

Thus, sitting atop a hierarchy of Uzbeki deserters, Turkestani brigands, Syrian carpetbaggers, retired Arab mercenaries, Kashmiri freedom fighters, Punjabi black sheep and an awestruck local population, these unholy young men, anointed by Mullah Omar, became Taliban.

These developments, when they were taking place, were not reaching everyone at the same speed. Local journalists had been silenced or bought off many decades ago. News travelled through official military press briefs or through word of mouth. All actors had only a part of the picture.

But all actors had to act.

So the first thing all actors tried to do was to develop their own eyes and ears in the area. The Chinese, the Russians, the Germans, the Indians, the British, the Israelis, the Saudis, the Iranians and of course the Americans, all had a stake in this war and their secret services began acquiring assets who could report to them on what was going on. The Chinese were hunting for Uighurs and

Turkomans. The Russians were looking for Uzbeks and Chechens. The Germans were looking for German Muslim converts being trained in these parts. The Indians were on the hunt for Kashmiri separatists. The Israelis were looking for Jordanians and Egyptians. The Iranians were looking for Jundullah and other anti-Shia groups. The Saudis, together with the Americans, were looking for Osama's al-Qaeda. It would have been a comedy had it not been so serious.

With so much competition, we kept losing our hard-earned agents to better-heeled foreign intelligence shops.

Everyone was groping for the script of this new war in our backyard, in Pakistan's backyard. The situation was extremely infuriating for us because we at that time were trying to manage a potent group of tribal scoundrels on Toyota 4x4s, the way we had placated other such groups before them—without fighting them. We needed to find a way for the marauders to settle down in their allotted spaces, to force them to make do with the revenue they got from local taxes without disrupting everyone else's gravy train. We worked frantically to cobble together the new Taliban into patchwork alliances using funds and threats, but if you threatened too aggressively they would kidnap an army troop on patrol. If you paid or persuaded one group to lie low, another would take their place, asking for their share.

Confused and demoralized, we genuinely thought the whole world was conspiring against us. Rule Number 1 now seemed a national motto.

Forced by circumstance, unable to buy out all the rascals at once, we too began to pick and choose. Tentatively, not knowing which rascal was already an agent for some other outfit, we began favouring some rascals as our own. These were called the good rascals. They were selected based on various common sense criteria. A Pashtun rascal was better than a Tajik rascal. A Kandahari Pashtun was better than a Kabuli Pashtun. A Sunni Kandahari was better than a Shia Kandahari. A Sunni with a cousin in the army was better than a Sunni with a cousin working for an NGO. And so on.

Thus began a turf war between these good and bad rascals in our FATA belt. And my cousin, Major Zayn, hunkered down with his knife and waited for an order to fight. The rest of the world pieced together information gleaned from Kabuli, Shia Tajiks to understand what the hell was going on.

It is at this point that two war allies realized they were allies no more. Intertwined supply routes still kept the US and Pakistan together on the surface, but underneath they began looking at each other as enemies.

And we became pariahs for the world. All for control of a few upstart rascals on 4x4s.

This is called the fog of war.

But you can call it Rule Number 1.

Waiting for Night to Fall

OUTSOURCE crashed when the first bombs began to fall on Kandahar. My first frantic call from a frayed customer in America came in while I was on my way to my wedding. I never had the courage, though, to admit this to your mother or to mine, Hyder. Bombs rained in Afghanistan and order cancellations bombed my inbox. It cannot last, I told myself. We will bounce back, I hoped. Then, our investment house pulled out too. Yet I kept things to myself and started ploughing all my savings into salaries hoping for business to return. I soon lost everything. Everything.

To a new wife, I had no words to explain what had just happened. This was not part of my destiny. But it was now who I was. Broken, bitter and reclusive.

Thus began another journey.

The tale of it cannot be told without first speaking of my friend Khawaja Imran.

I first met Khawaja Imran in a cold and damp junior school washroom in second grade, where I had gone for the first time in my life in a real emergency. Khawaja stood at the sink with his thick legs, khaki knickers and a round face. He pointed accusingly to the floor. An accident he was convinced was my doing. I turned to look, trying to explain my innocence. Khawaja did not buy it; but then suddenly and quietly and smoothly turned accusation into complicity and walked out of the door. Such was the power of his suggestion that I still cannot decide if I was responsible for that accident or not. He had this gift, a knack for making himself available at the worst possible time, of turning things around to make the sublime ordinary, the surreal routine. He has appeared on my doorway or on our verandah or in my rear view mirror again and again and again throughout my life.

And when OutSource collapsed, I found him one day, standing at my bedroom door.

Khawaja insisted that we move quickly. 'Where? To do what?' I asked. He did not know himself, but he did not let me know that.

'We will start a new business.' He said. 'You are an engineer after all. We will start an engineering business.'

'But I only processed data.'

'Then we will process data,' he said. 'We will do anything,' and he filled my head with ideas and my lungs with oxygen. 'What can you do?'

I thus began every day with waking myself up and proceeding to his family's business office in Alfalah building on the Mall to literally do anything that we could. The Khawaja family bought a computer they put on the conference-cum-dining table and that was my desk for the next two years.

It took me a month to realize that the Khawaja family business was itself bankrupt. Having seen dizzying heights in trading cotton and making garments, they too were forced to suddenly sell everything in a bad deal and were exactly in the same spot as I was. But they were the bravest, most colourful lot of brothers I had ever seen. I soon realized that the computer they had bought for me was, at that time, a major investment for them.

And thus we began again, wounded and desperate.

I brought home no salary and never bought anything for your mother. I was moody and on edge, and I could not explain what my plan was.

For our plan changed every day. We simply tried everything.

Khawaja's brother had friends who owned sugar mills. We developed a plan to supply cheaper power to them. We researched the alternatives, made a presentation and tried to explain to them how to make sugar more efficiently. It did not work out.

The World Bank had financed research at Harvard that called for all census records of Pakistan and India before and after partition to be computerized. We got the contract but had no money to rent an office big enough to get the work done. Desperation can lead to excellent economies. I talked to Shaheena, the brilliant technician who had once kept all the computers in OutSource working. She was excited enough by our order to convert her family home behind the Secretariat building that was once the French garrison into a sudden data entry centre for Harvard and the World Bank. With the advance payment received from Harvard, we bought second-hand Y2K rejected computers and built a small remnant of OutSource on borrowed tables and chairs between the kitchen and the lounge, separated from the living area by a bed sheet hung from hooks.

Shaheena soon put together a crack team of part-timers who manned the stations 24/7. Some were students, some used to work as office boys in the day, but most were women who lived in the area and suddenly were able to earn good money from solid work. The area was so thickly populated that no one had to walk more than a few minutes to reach the office. Everyone had been referred by someone else already working in the office. Purdah was not an issue. Quality control systems were made, payment methods to the workers were devised based on characters-entered and accuracy-achieved. Halfway through the project, a team came to check and I took them through Shaheena's home, dodging laundry in balconies hung out to dry. They found neatly stacked documents, whirring hard drives and fingers moving professionally on keyboards in a place where Shaheena and her mother and her nine siblings also lived.

It was fantastic.

The Board of Revenue keeps land records on large registers and even larger maps made on huge swaths of rugged cloth. Large bribes are paid to the patwaris who are able to read this very logical but antiquated database. The system was ripe for developing an electronic database and we knew we could do this. We tried but could not break the thick veil of government.

Harvard followed up the first project with another one requiring that all company records in the Securities and Exchange Commission of Pakistan—the SECP—be computerized.

Shaheena's operation was amazing—simple, effective and

amazing. We rented a photocopier to copy all the records at the SECP. Shaheena arranged for some of her friends who understood balance sheets to supervise the operation. But the SECP would not agree. How could they send all of Pakistan's company data to a foreign country? Why did it need computerization in the first place? This roadblock was crossed by getting a Pakistani university involved. And data entry started. Until one day when I got a call from Shaheena that our entry into the SECP was suddenly banned. I went over and was faced with a suspicious veil of official silence. Our entry was banned by the head of all heads. I had to make more subtle inquiries. Our livelihood rested on finding a solution but first I had to find where the problem lay.

I went to the only man in the whole office who actually worked—the librarian. He was the one who retrieved files all day without air conditioning while all the heads sat in cool carpeted offices making sure all the records of all the companies were kept in the library. He told me that in the night, the janitor had picked up a large stash of boxed SECP files and had sold them to a recycling operation for hard cash. Having found the problem, I was able to sell our solution. We already had copies and computerized records of what had gone missing and finally it dawned on the heads what we were trying to do. We got tea and biscuits whenever we asked after that.

These sporadic victories kept us going.

We researched the new laws about making electricity from canal heads, but it was not feasible.

Khawaja's brother explained how a garment manufacturing unit could be automated, so we made a partnership arrangement with a small software firm to support our back end while I went forward to sell the concept to Angora Textiles. We spent weeks mapping the process and designing a solution. Fifty rupees worth of petrol got me to Angora and another fifty got me back. Every day those hundred rupees were an investment—a risk—and every day we had to decide whether to invest more. Angora did not know this. For them I was a brilliant, successful and well-groomed solution to all their problems.

In the end, Angora did not buy what we proposed. But I began to understand the power of image. I had spent a lifetime finding finite solutions to finite problems. Khawaja Imran, however, existed beyond the finite. He lived on emotions and breathed feelings; he loved humans and everything that made us fallible. He studied expressions and body language, and lived to make an impression. He could read the feelings held close within the hearts of men and could move them not only with grand actions but also with simple impressions and subtle choices. He spent hours deciding the colour of a tie best suited to an occasion. And he could be the humblest of god's pious servants—depending on the need of the hour. A man exactly the opposite of me. But he taught me the impact an impact can make. Without any money in our pockets, he taught me, image was all we could trade with and that is what we did.

One day, during a particularly trying month, I got a call that Zia Chishty wanted to see me. Handsome, young, well-educated and successful, Zia Chishty was a man of his time. He had graduated from Columbia and Stanford, and had launched a unique new firm that had been listed on

NASDAQ, with a back office in Pakistan. He was simply phenomenal. With a few Harvard MBAs in tow, he had swept through Pakistan with millions of dollars in venture capital and had taken bold decisions to expand and grow, exciting young Pakistanis in his wake. Only imagination imposed any limits on this man. With the initial success of his back office, he bought a large block of land outside Lahore next to an unused railway station and contracted with the railways to run his own rail service from Lahore to this suburb—bussing young minds back and forth on his own rented line as efficiently as possible. His company was what OutSource had wanted to be. His company also had had to shut its Pakistani operations after 9/11 and had shifted to Costa Rica. The thousands of bright men and women, who were suddenly laid off, could not understand such a decision. But international finance makes very quick decisions and the whole dream had left Pakistan as swiftly as it had entered.

When I got a call from Zia Chishty that dry October, not many people knew he was in Pakistan. Not many people knew his plans, but he was optimistic that business would return to Pakistan soon. So he had diverted some of his money back in hopes of starting a new, but smaller, operation. Here was a man that I had only read about and dreamt of being like some day, and he wanted to meet me. I went over to his operation at night and found that he was a man like me. He sat in jeans and sweatshirt on a borrowed table and did not wear a crown or even a Rolex. He did not drive a flashy car and was, in fact, as simple a man as any—with millions of dollars in stocks. He came straight to the point.

He wanted to start a transcription business and wanted me to work for him. He would pay me more in a month than I was hoping to make in a year. But there was one catch. We would look for business together and I would be paid only if we won some business. I was mesmerized. He was waiting for a phone call from America where we could make a sale even that night, and he showed me a presentation he was working on for that phone call right there. And then, to wait for the phone call we went down to Abbott Road and had a cup of tea by the roadside, and I was amazed that this man prayed and thanked Allah for the cup of tea before he drank it. I wanted to work for this man. Had our prayers been answered? Was this the revival of OutSource? Would my team be back to work with more work than they could handle? Zia did not need me to answer. We returned to his office. I participated in the phone call and I was sold. Emails came and went and I could see international business being transacted the way it should be.

It took me a few weeks to realize that a month had passed and that the month was still as dry and unforgiving as the last. It was then that I truly realized that I was not Zia Chishty. I was married and my wife was expecting a child. My company was bankrupt, not his. I could not take the risks that he could. Time was all I had to invest and if I spent it wrongly, I would not be able to survive. I quickly climbed back down to earth to scrounge for something on the ground—not in the air. Dreams of boyhood stood in one corner and the image of a successful businessman stood dejected in another as I waited for night to fall and then to make the call to America. I loaded money into my cell phone and dialled. Zia was in his car on a highway in LA when he took my call and I explained to him my decision not to continue. He was very angry. And I thought that was absolutely great. He felt betrayed and let down, and I could not explain myself on phone that I was trying to be as professional as possible. He let me have it and I could only mumble. Your mother sat with me in the darkened room, listening. And that was that.

LA was suddenly in another world.

The next morning I woke myself up and made my way back to Alfalah building.

White Technologies

KHAWAJA Imran wanted me to meet Waheed Gul. Gul was a political worker. But of late, with political activity brought to a close by martial law, he had found work making seats for motorcycles. He made them and supplied them to Qingqi Motorcycle Company. Qingqi's motorcycle rickshaw was a phenomenon. He could introduce us to the procurement clerk. Khawaja and I looked at each other. The carpet in Khawaja Imran's office was beginning to fray at the edges. 'Do you want to be a partner?' we asked Waheed Gul. But Qingqi would need some references. We had a classmate whose family made tractor gears. We asked him if he too wanted to be a partner.

And together we all made our way to Qingqi.

Mr Wei sat in one corner of the factory perspiring but cool, and handed us an axle shaft, which the engine rotates and which, in turn, rotates the two back wheels of a rickshaw. 'This keeps breaking in the field,' he said. 'We pay two hundred rupees for each shaft. If you can make something stronger for ₹175, the order is yours.'

Khawaja's brother named the venture White Technologies.

We began to first deconstruct and then reconstruct the

shaft. We realized quickly that the existing shaft was made from cheap grade iron. If we used more expensive Pakistan Steel grade iron, we would need less iron, and we could also design it based on known characteristics of that grade. Then we realized that the gears on the existing shaft were not made by a proper gear hobber but by simply cutting splines into the shaft. As these splines were irregular, they never exactly fit into the wheel sprocket and that led it to fail. Also, the gear skin was hardened using a gas torch. If we could harden the skin using electrical current, we could harden each gear tooth to the right depth, keeping its core soft and malleable. Finally, we realized the shaft did not need to be as thick. We could use a much thinner and lighter shaft if we just welded a sleeve on one edge where it needed to be thick to accommodate the bearing. If everything worked according to plan, we could actually make a shaft, not only stronger, but lighter and costing us only a hundred rupees. We could make a killing. But first it had to be made. So we went to buy our first rod of high grade steel, one inch thick.

The iron market of Lahore is its real heart. Tons and tons of steel are recycled, rolled, imported and fashioned just north of the walled city, along the railway line. Large oxen pull wooden carts made to carry tons of iron billets to steel yards where the billets are poured into house-like furnaces and then reshaped into rods of different shapes and strengths. Traders stock and hoard, keeping an eye on international markets through the Internet while broken ships are trucked all the way to Lahore from the seafronts to be melted down. The roads are all reinforced concrete hidden under dust, the air smells of a sweet aroma that emanates from the casting sand and the air is hot and hands are thick and men are manly. Here, Khawaja Imran sat in a glass cubicle office and explained that he had brought with him the greatest mechanical engineer produced by America and that I was working on a revolutionary product for the automobile industry while I hunkered outside in the yard over a single twenty-foot rod of steel with a vernier caliper in hand. I knew how a vernier worked in principle but had never really had to use it. Slowly, peering intently through my glasses, careful not to let the sweat on my brow trickle onto the lens, I worked with the caliper to make sure the rod was actually an inch thick and regular. Not only did I not know how to use a caliper, we also did not have the money to buy another rod if we got it wrong. In the meantime, Khawaja Imran tried hard to explain what was taking me so long as he negotiated a rate not just for the one rod but for a subsequent bulk rate that was sure to come as soon as the brilliant engineer from America finalized his excellent design for the automotive industry.

Now, having bought the twenty-foot steel rod, we could not carry it to our office. So we simply asked the steel yard to deliver it to a barring shop across the street. And they did. This is what is so fantastic about an eastern bazaar. The whole supply chain, with a choice of vendors for each link in the chain, is all arrayed in a small cluster interconnected with simple financial relationships.

The barring shed owns one machine that performs the almost superhuman job of squeezing steel (without heat) through a very hard ring, reducing the rod in diameter, making it longer, and giving it a regular shape and a tough skin. Like plasticine, steel is pulled through these rings by massive chains and pulleys across a long yard, and the result—if the chains are not broken—is a delectable, oil-immersed rod of steel shaped exactly to your desired size. After elongating and squeezing the rod—this process also stretches the skin of the steel in a way that makes it stronger for use—the barring shed will also cut the rod to the size you want using a bandsaw.

The next job was to machine the rods according to Qingqi's drawing on a lathe. But the best lathe machinists are not found in the iron market. For them, one must move along the rail tracks, closer to the railway workshops. These workshops were one of the largest in the British Raj, servicing all the northern railways with machinists whose fathers and grandfathers used to work here and who inherited the art of metalworking in their blood. Entire neighbourhoods are dedicated to metalworking in one form or another. The men here are more precise and smaller than the men in the iron market—more philosophical, more cerebral. Here, close to the Shalimar Gardens, in a side street that snakes through a kilometre of bazaar, we found a machinist more precise and more cerebral than the others. His machining was almost perfect. He would use a caliper where others would use a thumb. He could read a drawing easily and was soft spoken. His Punjabi was incongruously flawless but he was called Bhai Saab by everyone, a name more Urdu than Punjabi and a man more professional than the place around him. It was very difficult to tell that he was not from here and he tried very hard to keep low-key. I asked him but he did not tell me anything.

Much much later, he told me, slowly, as we waited for electricity one evening, lovingly feeling the smooth bevel of a freshly cut gear.

He was from India, from Delhi, from the old part, from a mohalla right next to the Red Fort, he told me. Technical education in India was better than in Lahore and that was why he was different.

But what was he doing here?

The Indian army had made parts of the Red Fort into a military base and the Mujahideen wanted to access it. Bhai Saab and his brothers had spent their childhood playing inside the fort and knew exactly what it looked like. So he and his brother drew them a map and then when an attack plan was made, the brothers helped the Mujahideen enter and then escape the Red Fort. The attack was one of the more spectacular accomplishments of the Mujahideen. His brother, Bhai Saab told me, then joined the cause and was part of the group that later attacked the Indian parliament, during which he was killed. Bhai Saab had since then been wanted by Indian intelligence and had found refuge here. Alone, gaunt, with a smoke hanging from his lip, Bhai Saab wore trousers and a shirt, and stood over his domain with the command of a winning captain. His team of distillated urchins, eager to learn, excited to create works of exquisite beauty and mathematics, oblivious to the drama, happy to step into his domain that stretched from a graveyard being encroached by eager seminary socialists on the one side and a sewage-filled plot of land navigable only by the fleet of foot on the other; a proud sanctuary of the mathematical arts, confident and vigorous. He is still the best machinist I know.

The rods were so shipped from one process to the next. Sleeves were fitted on, welded and grinded. Gears were cut and electrically heated. And two sample shafts were delivered to Qingqi for testing. A rickshaw was fitted with our shafts and put on the road. A month later, we had the order.

Now came the time to make a workshop and buy machines.

Necessity again helped us make the right decision. Rather than bringing machines to White Technologies, White Technologies would go to the machines. Rather than hiring the best craftsman, White Technologies would contract with the best craftsman, pay him more than anybody else, help him work better, check his quality, and still come out with the best and cheapest shaft that Qingqi could buy.

White Technologies would be a company that would market, design and sell shafts, but it would not make them. For this outlandish model to work, we had to make sure that we check our quality at each step.

Quality is best checked by measuring the dimensions of a worked piece to make sure it is within the required tolerance allowed by the design. But measuring each dimension with calipers and tape measures is not only cumbersome but also never reliable enough. The key is to build gauges in such a way that a machined part can fit inside such a gauge, only if it has the correct dimensions. Thus a gauge should not only be made accurately but also be cleverly designed in order to make it easy for the quality checker to use it repeatedly.

These gauges need to be ten times more accurate than the machined parts they must check. Men who make such gauges are thus even more precise and smaller than machinists. And such men are few and far between. Such men are highly paid for the works of art they produce but such works are not needed every day. So these men develop quirks that must be negotiated if you are to get them to do what you want.

Maulvi Rafiq was one such man. Emaciated, slight, with a scraggly beard snaking shyly below his chin, Maulvi Rafiq kept the cleanest, smallest, most organized workshop in Lahore. He worked in secret with the shutter of his workshop closed. The workshop kept mysterious hours because he could work any time during day or night. Before cell phones, the best way to reach him was to go to his home and to tell one of his nine school-going children that he was needed. He would then call you and arrive at your office with the efficiency of a Swiss watch. He had no patience for people who did not value time and no matter how important the customer, he would refuse to work for them if they were not there at the appointed time. He would quote outrageous prices and then, if you tried to negotiate, would disappear for months. If he loved anything more than his science or his nine children, it was Prophet Mohammad. And yet he would tell me, in whispered confidence, that Christians had much stronger faith than Muslims.

One day, a miracle almost took place on one of the golden nights of the Muslim calendar. He had gone, on that most auspicious of nights, with one of his sons, to hear a concert of hymns and *naats* at a vast gathering of the faithful. At the end of the gathering a lottery was held. You could participate in the lottery by simply putting a copy of your ID card in a big bowl. All the participants had eagerly entered the lottery because the grand prize was a return ticket to Mecca. Eventually the time came for the grand draw. With bated breath, the audience waited to hear the name of the winner. The announcer, speaking in fluent Arabicized Urdu, almost stumbled midway into the name but then read it through. 'Patrick...Patrick Massey', he read out and the crowd fell silent. This was obviously a mistake. How could a Christian be present here? The organizers quickly asked the announcer to take out another card and the bowl was brought forward again. But in this hushed commotion, a distant figure started moving to the stage saying that he was Patrick Massey and that he had won fair and square. At this point a frenzy took over the stage as agitated organizers moved to scuttle the obvious conspiracy. How could a Christian claim a prize for a pilgrimage to Mecca? He would just sell the ticket and pocket the money. What was he doing here anyway, some asked, one goes to Mecca only when called by the Almighty. Patrick Massey replied strongly that he was the chauffeur for one of the participants and had simply put his ID card into the bowl.

Amid such agitation, a cry rose among the faithful, who were now witnessing a miracle taking place before their very eyes. They shouted at the organizers not to argue with the Christian. The Almighty had indeed called him to Mecca they said. This was a miracle. The auspicious night and their hymns were now culminating in this most bizarre of Allah's actions. A Christian was being called to the Right Path. It suddenly became clear to the congregation that this young man had been chosen by Allah to be converted to Islam.

Eyes teared up and brothers in Islam were enthralled because they could see a miracle of conversion taking place and they were all playing a role in it. Cries of 'Allahu Akbar!' resounded across the four streets of the intersection where this congregation had gathered.

But the night again took a turn. Patrick Massey refused to convert. He only wanted the prize. Could he not see the Lord working through this lottery to reach his heart? A cold despair whispered through the crowd. Brave and affluent Muslims then began to raise the ante. They could see God's plan and they jumped to help out. A shopkeeper offered ten thousand rupees to the Christian if he converted. The announcer too understood God's message and Patrick Massey's predicament. Soon the prize for conversion had been supplemented by a hundred thousand rupees and the congregation was again abuzz. It was a time of solemn remembrance and sacrifice.

But Patrick Massey refused to become a Muslim. He simply wanted what he had fairly won. The congregation then solemnly drew another name from the lot and thrashed Patrick for causing such grief.

Maulvi Rafiq dropped his voice to a whisper. 'Any Muslim would have converted at this point,' he said. 'All he had to do was to say that he had converted and pocket the prize. There was no chance that another Christian was there in that gathering to report him. Why did he not convert?

Because he had much stronger faith.'

Maulvi Rafiq had named his nine children after the companions of the Prophet and it helped that his eldest was also named Omar. Of course, it also helped that prayer was very strictly observed in the office of the Khawaja family, and that Khawaja Imran and all his brothers supported beards and could recite the Quran better than many Saudis. Maulvi Rafiq therefore made concessions for us that he would not have for lesser mortals and we received the most strange-looking pieces of shiny oiled metal wrapped in old newspapers, which would somehow snuggle around different dimensions of our product, checking each process of production to the last micron.

This is a lesson I learnt from Khawaja Imran's family. Businesses are run by men, not by machines. One must understand men and their capabilities and then one must inspire them to do what they do best—for you. Leaders can excite their teams to do this in small businesses with personal effort. In large organizations, leaders must institute processes that force other team leaders to do the same.

With the quality check process in place, White Technologies simply focused on logistics and tracking and sweat, and packed shafts eventually emerged after having made their way across the city, to the Qingqi factory. None of our competitors could find out how we made these shafts because no one could find our factory. To the great consternation of these competitors, and as a final Khawaja Imran touch, the shafts were individually wrapped in plastic and then shipped to Qingqi in purpose-built wooden crates.

One day the man who made the crates came to me

and said happily that he would no longer be making them. They had rented out their yard to a Pathan, he told me. The yard in which his family had been woodworking for two generations would now make the family thirty thousand rupees a month. They could thus make more from the rent than they could from the work and they were now all going to retire from carpentry and find some decent work. These were strange times. The triply-mortgaged US property boom had jumped across the Atlantic, made its way to Dubai and snaked its way to this carpenter. We were at that time in an unprecedented boom despite the war. Property was increasing in value and price every day, and people were becoming millionaires without having to produce anything tangible. The richest men in Pakistan were becoming richer even as they closed down their factories. Rather than running a business with workers and taxes and hassles, the richest Pakistanis—like this carpenter—were better off shutting down factories and instead buying stock and real estate. These were strange times. Investors had a hard time deciding which property to invest in—which plot would give the most return. Those questions, though, were not for us because we had no money to invest.

We were giddy nonetheless. We had cash flow. We had made it back from the edge.

In Search of a Hero

When you have money, even a little money, the world begins to look different. The spine uncurls a bit, the knees uncoil more easily, and you begin to notice people as your equal—without hunger, without want. You begin to feel useful again.

You may still choose to shave with a bar of soap but the knowledge that you could walk into a store and buy shaving foam—if you so wanted—is all the fuel you need to be equal to any man.

You look at the world around you.

And you begin to argue, to fight for what you believe is right.

∞

A dark vine covers the window.
Light seeps through leaves,
Pushed against its will,
onto paper that sits before me.
A muezzin clears his throat.
A helicopter swoops overhead.
The pen of distant years,
In my hand, feels like lead.

I had given up the world of paper and pen as the last vestige of a forgotten youth and had delved headlong into a world of commerce, which for me had meant the hard, unforgiving company of steel, dust and blazing gases. The company of friends was replaced by friends of the company, the glint of ideals by the chink of capital. What mattered really did not matter.

But then, somehow, it was 2007 and I found myself at the stroke of midnight, perched at the edge of a makeshift roof—together with strangers who reminded me of my youth—waiting for a distant cavalcade to arrive. We drank tea until it lasted and then water until it ran out. We enjoyed a light breeze and the song and dance show that followed the arrival of each delegation. The lawyers from Pakpattan came with drums, and the lawyers from Abbottabad came wrapped in comic slogans; Jalib and Faiz mixed with Iqbal and bearded men danced into the night. It was a party until the sun came out.

The sun hit those on the roof first—and the wait became longer. Rumours and gossip, among the few who had found their way to this only vantage point, which peered into the High Court, ebbed away as the numbers began to thin. We lost many at that point as those last few hours stretched away and the sun cut into our skin.

After ten hours on the roof, there was a swell. I held onto the edge. My boots wedged against the narrow ledge. My hands held onto a crevice for security as the sun roasted my body. The crowd knew it was at the edge but more came to peer over shoulders. The front row crouched with me and peered over the four-storey drop, and each onlooker negotiated into position. A jeep had entered the crowd below. I looked around gingerly. Where had I got myself trapped? I could have seen this on TV.

'*O sher da bacha*,' someone said and a moustachioed man in a dark suit stood out from the jeep's sunroof. We clapped and clapped. Smiles all round.

'This government is gone for sure,' one said.

'This is a new Pakistan,' said another.

'After 1940, this is the biggest day in our history,' said another as Blackberrys mixed with Sanyos and Italian leather crushed against chappals. Men with beards danced with men waving red flags.

In the tumult of Musharraf's waning decade, his chief justice—who would not have been chief justice had it not been for Musharraf's coup, who had become chief justice because he had taken an oath to abide by military rules when Musharraf had taken over—had suddenly refused to resign. He—Iftikhar Chaudhry—was now the champion of every champion of rule of law in Pakistan. In trying to save his job, this man, with dubious credentials and a streetfighter's strong will, was now our enemy's enemy and therefore our hero.

Suddenly all the night's political gossip coalesced into one single defining challenge. The moustachioed chief justice had changed the debate of liberal versus conservative, of right versus left, of pro-West versus anti-West, to one issue and one alone: the right of man to rule over men versus the right of laws to rule above all. We were then under Musharraf's law and this choice was getting lost in the weekly bomb blasts, which had only just begun, and in the exploding stock market, which was zooming up, and real estate, which was doubling in value every few years.

This choice was thus not an easy one because when we said no to the rule of a few men we also said no to Musharraf's years of growth and to Western patronage. We said no to the status quo. We said yes to the uncontrolled force of common men. Sensible men found it difficult choosing sides on this issue because so much was at stake for sensible men.

This choice threw the theory of clash of civilizations into the sea. This choice said that the world's tussle was not between two civilizations, was not between Islam and the West, but between the civilized and the uncivilized. The human race was one civilization and the fight was only at its edges; between those who wanted to be a part of this civilization and those who were not yet ready for it. This choice said that a liberal dictator cannot be an ally of the West because he is a force on the wrong edge of this one civilization; a dictator is a force resisting this one civilization as much as the jihadi outliers. This, therefore, was not an easy choice for the West as well.

But a tantalizing choice it was. A choice that brought me to the edge of a roof, forcing me to rethink the choices I have made as a boy and then as a man—the choice between practical commerce and the dirty ideals of policy. It forced me to think of a choice my father had to make three decades earlier under another martial law, when he was a judge. I shoved my way back through the crowd, hungry for breakfast, hungry to talk, the weight of choice heavy on my shoulders. I cannot choose the destiny of other men but I can choose how I look at the world and how I think. As I walked home through the empty streets of Lahore, hungry and thirsty, choices became easier. Hunger makes hands shake and connects men where they all become the same. And ideals melt.

As I reached back and joined you for breakfast and tried to explain what I had seen, I realized strangely that this was just another Sunday. The paper was late as always, the tea was spilled on the table. Breakfast was a chore for your mother. Ben10 on TV was more important for you. The world, for those who were not on that roof, was still the same.

∞

But you must understand. The law for us is not just an abstraction.

My father was a judge. An honest judge. Famed for his quick grasp of matters, for his amazing ability to politely listen, smilingly disagree, quickly decide and conscientiously write more judgments than anyone else on the bench.

After he earned his law degree, he was selected in the government's elite corps of managers who managed districts and police, but he opted to go into the High Court, shunning the immense power of the bureaucracy of that time for a lower profile assignment.

And then, the world...had turned. There was no CNN then to tell us that it was turning, but it was. In one fateful year—1979—the Shah of Iran was overthrown by Khomeini, the staff of the American embassy in Tehran were taken hostage, a thousand Saudi soldiers died in Mecca in a battle to win back the Kaaba from a rebel Mahdi, the US embassy in Pakistan was burned down by a mob and the Russians invaded Afghanistan. Dominoes were falling.

One man stood up. His name was Muhammad Zia-ul-Haq—General Zia. He had just hanged, by manipulating judicial process, our prime minister.

And so, in his early forties, as my father sat in his office in the High Court in Lahore one June morning, he received a phone call from the registrar. All judges were to report to the governor's house in an hour. The choice my father would now have to make was left unsaid by the caller but he knew then that a choice was upon him.

He would have to take again his oath of office. The words of the oath were innocuous but they would seal his acceptance that the courts could not challenge the dictates of General Zia. I was in school. My mother was in her college, teaching a class. My father's father was in his clinic in Gojra, peering into a farmer's eye. My father was then on his own, as men are when faced with choice. He was then the junior-most judge. He picked up the phone and dialled a senior, a mentor.

'What should we do?' *If anything needs to be done, it should be done together*, he thought.

'We must wait and see. Everyone has to take their own decision.'

Black Mazdas with chauffeurs in colonial white and judges in Zia's new black began leaving the gates of the High Court. Abu thought he would find out more when he reached the governor's house; he would read the words of the oath; he would discuss; he would have a choice. He did not know it then but he had already made his choice when he got into the car.

He thought he was contemplating a decision as the black Mazda curved out of the iron gate with the sharp spikes. His foot twitched with the pain he had once felt when one of these spikes had gone through his foot—in college.

He knew he would never agree to what he knew was wrong. But was his mind playing games? Legally, his mind kept telling him, he was only being asked to take oath again on the law of the land. The law of the land was crooked but the Supreme Court, not he, was empowered to judge the law. He could, through a resignation, signal his disdain for the law, but would his resignation mean anything? Would the lawyers strike at the resignation of the junior-most judge? Was the force of history tilted against him?

The car passed the Lawrence Gardens where he had won a tennis championship for his college the day his team, on their way back to the hostel, had decided to take a short cut through the lawns of the High Court many years ago, only to be chased out over the gate and its spikes. He saw the practice wall where I took my tennis lessons.

Then, in seconds, the gates of the governor's house were opened and colonels and brigadiers milled about tea settings and carbon copied documents and the judges who had arrived, looked at each other and tried to figure out who was missing. My father chose to do what he thought was right but felt was wrong.

Some of the most respected names in the field of law took oath that day, but some did not. The ones who did not take oath were relegated to a list of anonymous heroes, uncelebrated but quietly respected.

For our family, a schism opened that day. We were honest people, we worked hard, and we lived simply and merrily. What my father did was not illegal nor unexplainable, but from that day on we carried a burden that could not be undone. My father could never talk to me about it. All he said to my mother was that it was not yet time.

He did not know it then but time was one thing he did not have.

I know now that he made a difficult choice.

He chose to stay on and his choice meant that there was an honest judge on the bench. But his choice furthered the edict that some men—uniformed salaried men—are above the rule of law.

It is strange to think that rule of law was actually a choice.

Friendship

As democracy fought with the military and the military fought with phantoms and the phantoms fought with us, we all began to look for patterns in the shadows. We began, all of us, one by one, to leave the common courtyard of our nation. And we began looking for the corners—for safety at the edges. There was no middle ground any more.

∞

Maybe, having finally arrived back from the depths of bankruptcy, I started believing in myself more than I had for many years past. Maybe it was the world around me. Maybe I too was moving towards the edges, away from the middle? I do not know. I really do not know why I said what I said.

You see, one confident Sunday morning, I had gone to my friend Khawaja Imran's house and met his aging mother in the morning sun. It was Ramadan.

She asked me about my fasts and I told her I was not fasting. She asked after my health and I said I was fine. She asked if I was travelling and I told her no. Then she asked me, perplexed, why it was that I was not fasting and I told her that I did not. I explained to her that in fact many people in my family also did not.

Khawaja Imran's mother was incredulous. She had never heard of such disrespect of the scriptures. And I was a friend of her son? And I had brought my whole family into it as well? I was a most definite rotten apple. Neither her sons nor her husband could convince her otherwise. I had crossed the line. Decades of friendship were now going down the drain in front of my eyes.

Khawaja Imran and I tried very hard to undo this sudden turn of fortune, but my categorical statement had been too strong. No one could unsay it.

Then one day a cousin of my father's came trooping into our house. Whenever she comes to Lahore, she visits the three saints, and when you were a little long in coming, she had taken me and your mother to Daata Saab and had anointed my head with the oil of the blessed lamp. She was a professor and a frequent visitor to Khawaja Imran's mother. I explained to her what I had done—you see, she had seen how my father and his father before him had done such things in the past. She took me in tow and I sat with my head bowed as she apologized on my behalf and explained that though I had strayed I was being watched over and I would return to the right path soon and that I would keep my fasts the next year. Now it is exactly one year and I have kept my promise of fasting—for the wrong reasons—not for God, though God and I go back a few years, but for Khawaja, for he and I go back longer.

Naming the Taliban

I sat alone, facing the setting sun, troubled.

My arguments on FATA had yet again been rubbished, to a man, by my friends, and my friends represented the decision-making elite of Punjab. They were also the heartland. Yet again I was unable to convince them. My arguments had been quite lonely for quite some time now and I was used to this, but yesterday I had found support. I had corroboration. But no one believed my expert witness either.

The established argument in the plains was that the tribal way is more religious than the urban way and that the tribes of FATA are fighting to establish sharia; that the army was a tool of the West, being used by Western powers to quell this legitimate struggle.

The day before, having found a person from FATA brave enough to voice my stories and to speak with data and stats, I had been exhilarated that the truth would now be obvious for all to see. I had hurriedly gathered a gaggle of my friends, some of whom have a hand on the pulse of Punjab and can shape public opinion. I quickly introduced the researcher I had found and let go. I had been confident that finally the truth would dawn on them, my friends who had known me since elementary school but who had always dismissed my theories as radical Westernized rantings. When this researcher, a Pashtun, who came from much closer to the action, added facts to my theories, I was astounded. I had found another person like myself and thought the problem would now be solved and opinion would finally take a back seat to the truth.

But I was wrong.

My professor and his colleagues began the conversation and I waited—anxious and passionate—for my friends' opinions to change.

I saw instead how two worlds can collide despite the best of mutual intentions. Because both groups were equally emotional about their opinions, equally emotional about the outcomes and equally patriotic, the divide could not be bridged even an inch. No opinion even wavered, much less changed. I watched the discussion as it became tense without becoming belligerent and could feel it become pregnant with pain before both sides, in deference to each other, once they had judged the other's intractable position, backed down without any real confrontation. It was a perfect example of Eastern negotiation. Each side gave the other a way out but went home convinced that the other was misguided. What I could see as an obvious truth, my dearest friends and their brothers saw as an equally obvious fraud. I could not understand them and they could not understand me.

The fate of our country lay in the balance. Our discussion was not on an esoteric philosophical point but on the very real and gathering threats to the soul of our society.

The phone rang. It was my cousin, Zayn. A call from Lieutenant Zayn, Captain Zayn, Major Zayn—as he progressed through the ranks—would always break any conversation with his loud laugh and other-worldly stories, but today his call from Baluchistan's border with Iran was of no help. I explained my disappointment with my friends and he laughed again. 'People change their opinion only if they need you or if they are afraid of you.' He spoke like a soldier. 'You have never changed anyone's opinion in your life. Why start now?'

'Never?' I asked with a small laugh of my own.

'Okay, once.' He knew what I was referring to. His laugh could not conceal the irony of the situation. Thirty years ago, the family had decided that I was too timid and bookish, and it was agreed that my cousin Kami Bhai, ten years my senior, would be deputed to roughen up my edges. Family legend thus came into being that Kami Bhai had armed his air rifle and, with me in tow, had shot a parrot on the banks of the canal in Lahore. As he and I both then stared at the dead parrot, I asked him why he had killed it, but he had no answer. So, rather than me becoming a hunter, Kami put down his airgun and became a failed peacemaker.

Hence, I had changed someone's opinion—once.

'And today you do not want to make peace. You want to convince your friends to make war.' Zayn's laugh carried well over the airwaves.

'They will never listen,' Zayn said. 'Forget them and watch TV. Federer is playing Nadal in Melbourne.'

But I could not forget it.

Instead, like a widowed housewife, I began reassembling

the arguments from yesterday's fight, relishing each nuance, reliving each bit of expression until it was slowly recreated before my eyes, grimace upon sweet grimace. And I began noticing a pattern.

My friends had a clear attachment to the word *Taliban* that I did not feel. When I associated any atrocities with the Taliban, the conversation very quickly dried up, not that my friends doubted that atrocities were being committed. They simply could not imagine the Taliban would be committing them.

They did not associate the word with a fanatic gunman, as I did, but instead with a bygone golden era—of tranquillity, of justice, of law and order. This association is so strongly ingrained that it evokes the same images in them as does the age of the Rightly Guided Caliphs of our Islamiyat textbooks. Now, the atrocities we refer to are just as horrific for my friends as they are for me, but the very severity and depravity of these acts makes it impossible for my friends to have a discussion with anyone who can attribute them to such sanctified personages as the Taliban. The conversation had been a nonstarter from the beginning.

I quickly called Ali Hyder and got a confirmation. Yes, this really was the case, he said. And I knew I was onto something.

Ali Hyder is my best friend. I named you after him, Hyder, and he named his son after me. He is the sweetest, most truthful person I know. I remember when, fifteen years ago, he started sporting a small beard. I told him with God as our witness to shave it off and if there was any punishment for doing so, I would gladly take it for him, preferably in the next world. I explained to him how people react to beards and how people make fun of beards and I told him to trust me, to believe me, and that that day would be the first and last day that I would ask this of him as a friend. But he said he could not and soon his beard was a fistful. And that was that.

He clarified this mystery of the Taliban for me.

'They did not hurt anybody. They were living in peace and they were attacked. I do not agree with their version of Islam. But they brought equality and justice and pacified the whole of Afghanistan and freed the people from the warlords. They were uneducated and that was the best that they could do. They have no fight with Pakistan. But they were attacked because the world is afraid of such Islam. They are inconvenient for the West.'

My mind went back to the discussion of the previous night. 'How could men who do not have shoes to wear attack two buildings on the other side of the earth?' someone had asked.

Ali Hyder knew I was a sceptic and he wanted to break it to me gently, and I, for a change, wanted him to tell me, slowly, the whole story. As a thinking man himself, he too was not certain, he said, but he continued. 'The 9/11 attacks were planned as an excuse to enter Afghanistan and Iraq. There was not a single bomber who was either Iraqi or Afghani,' he said. 'So why attack Afghanistan? The Taliban had no idea where New York was on a map. It is a conspiracy against the only truly Islamic movement in the world, and the world ganged up and destroyed it.' Ali explained to me that all of our friends thought that I was too closely associated with the West to see things clearly and that I had bought into all the propaganda I see on television.

'What we see now,' he said, 'are further conspiracies designed to wean us away from the very concept of the Taliban. A corrupt and criminal gang of marauders have been trained to call themselves the Pakistani Taliban. These guys commit atrocities all over Pakistan and then take credit for them. Thus, having destroyed the government of the Taliban, the conspirators are now destroying the name of the Taliban according to a well-thought-out plan.'

It was the first time I had had the patience to listen to this whole argument without jumping in and arguing about it. And though I could not see the light, I could at least see why Ali and all my friends shook their heads every time I played into the hands of the conspirators—the Indians, the Jews and the Americans. The argument to him was watertight and there was no reason to doubt it.

Not for the first time in my life, rather than arguing I began looking for common ground.

I asked him about the two famous marauders then always in the news—Fazlullah of Swat and Baitullah of Waziristan. I asked him if it was insensitive of me to call these murderers Taliban, and he said, 'Yes.'

'Are they Indian agents?' I asked.

'Probably,' he said. Narrowing the field, I asked if I did not call Fazlullah a Taliban, would he agree with me that Fazlullah is a bad guy? He again agreed.

'Do you agree then that he should be eliminated?' He totally agreed.

Slowly the web began to unravel. We were on common ground. We agreed on killing a man.

But we had been fighting for the last two years on what to name him.

End of a Movement

THE air was clear and Lahore looked like Srinagar does in newspapers. Empty. Eerie. Waiting. I walked in grey—grey shirt and grey hair—through bright alleys, mapping the wanderings of my youth, surprised to find that alleys still connected as they did in my mind and got closer and closer to the High Court, ever conscious that the farther I walked, the more confident my step, the more incongruous a figure I became. The boys who saw me could not place me just as I could not place them. I left home to fight for the rule of law. They were fighting for kites. With apologetic eyes I passed through them, not knowing what to do with my hands. I emerged on the Mall.

It was 11 a.m., 27 May 2009. A cyclist flitted by. Several men stood in an alley. I turned right and began walking again. A police jeep sped towards me, sirens blazing, and then passed. A phalanx of policemen blocked Regal Chowk and I hesitated. Instead of moving forward, I stood in the centre of the chowk, as if on holiday. Just stood there. Inspectors checked their constables and intelligence men talked on radios and policemen joked as stragglers asked to be let onto the chowk. I stood with my hands on my hips, realizing that they could not understand who I was and were probably as scared of me as I was of them. I folded my hands as the radios signalled an approaching mob from an empty Hall Road. The policemen redeployed and readied themselves. I moved into the shade of a tree and waited for the mob. No one questioned my presence.

A European couple, each with dirty blond hair, arrived from the other side. The man was in a saffron pajama suit and a thick Nehru jacket and dreadlocks made into a bun. The woman had wrapped herself in layers of scarves and shawls. What was this world coming to? The policemen looked at them and then at me. I nodded and they were forced to intercede. 'The Americans will try anything,' one said. 'Check his jacket,' said another. One man moved forward, reciting verses, not knowing what fate had in store for him.

'Stop them,' I said, unfolding my hands. And then I simply sauntered past the police in the centre of the road. I was through. When I had made it halfway to the next intersection, fifteen men carrying signs stormed the police from Hall Road and grappled with them, throwing them back and running through. Men peering from the alleys clapped and I moved forward as the protesting men waited for reinforcements from the rear. The High Court waited in the next intersection with another phalanx of police.

A lone character wearing nothing but shorts sat on the main balcony of the Commercial Building and clapped constantly as I passed him.

The police stood shoulder to shoulder across the road. But between the last shoulder and the footpath along the edge of the road was a tree. I began walking slowly toward

End of a Movement • 155

it and the police began asking me who I was. I mumbled authoritatively as I walked. They asked me for a badge but I kept walking until I reached the gap and then two of them scampered around the tree. I told them just as grimly to look behind me. A mob was approaching and if they touched me I would break their legs. They threatened me to go back but no one touched me and I passed through again. Now I was inside.

I was getting used to this. It felt good to feel powerful.

༺༻

When I had woken that morning, the second Long March had been stopped, the Lawyers' Movement with it. All its leaders had been detained or sent home. The roads were silent. Hope was lost. As I showered and shaved, I thought what it might have been like and then put on my running shoes and a grey shirt. I kissed your cheek as you sat watching Ben10, running a fever, too busy to notice me. I did not tell your mother and did not know what the consequence of this useless decision might be. I then slipped out the door quietly. Whether the leaders showed up or not, I was going to be there. Whether it made a difference or not, I felt numb. I thought about bombs and useless gestures and knew that you would not forgive me if I did not return that day.

༺༻

At eleven-thirty, when the crowd was very thin, the first

two tear gas shells dropped and we got a taste of what was to come. A mad dash for water and then we were back and feeling satisfied. At every moment, the thought of a suicide bomb was palpable and I thought again and again of my decision to be there. As the crowd swelled past noon, a carnival of desperate hope seemed under way. Our mental pictures of a glorious Long March stretching from Lahore to Gujranwala were supplanted by the reality of a single intersection full of unorganized hoarse throats shouting and innocent eyes staring at one another searching for suicide jackets.

A movement was lost, however. We had come here in desperation—not victory. The smell of failure, like rotten flesh, made our nostrils twitch and we looked at the maulvis with their thick sticks and at the jeans-clad activists in baseball caps and at the might of the state that stood guard over our liberties and our anger mounted. Men challenged policemen with taunts to their manhood and others tried to stop them. I cursed the powers of the world that were colluding in their silence with the baton rather than with the tear gas-soaked dupatta. The crowd swelled past one o'clock and TV cranes hung over the crowd and reporters kept moving through us, excited, conscious and exaggerating.

At two o'clock, the crowd had fully choked the intersection and was now spilling out onto the four streets, yet one could easily stand in the crowd or walk half a minute off to a lone fruit vendor, eat a banana for ten rupees or an orange for five, and then rejoin the crowd to find it throbbing to different beats. As the crowd milled around this way, the clear lines between the police and the crowd grew more and more confused. The jamaat were ready for a fight. The police knew that they were running out of time. Then two more shells were fired and the crowd began to run—more from each other than from the shell. When a crowd runs, it asks for no direction and choosing to stand your ground is not an option. Your biggest enemy is suddenly not the police or the shell but the crowd that will crush you if you do not move with it.

This was not the first time I stood while a crowd ran. I stood my ground—behind a traffic pole—and could see the faces as they fled with glee before the gas cloud could engulf them. In what seemed like half a second, the intersection was empty and I stood alone with a couple of gas canisters for company. I had seen on TV people pick these up and throw them back. Here was my chance. Like a fielder in first slip, I could catch this one without moving my feet. As I moved for it, the canister hit me in the nose and in the eye. My body came instinctively into action and I ran with my eyes closed and new shells began to fall, and when I opened my eyes to get my bearings, a man threw up white paste and others then dragged him away. I reached a tap only to find it mobbed, so I followed old pictures in my brain guiding me to another one—outside a building where I had thirty years ago seen my first pair of glasses being ground at E. Plomers, Opticians—and splashed water into my eyes and breathed.

That day, as I said, was the last day of the Lawyers' Movement. In one day the movement was crushed. The Long March was decimated in countless such baton-charges across the country. The leaders of the movement never left their districts.

But then, in another setting, at the home of Musharraf's original nemesis—the prime minister he had sent into exile, the only leader after Benazir's death who could challenge the established order—a drawing room was growing pensive. Millionaires with Rolex watches and white clothes were being forced to play a hand they were not designed for. With bulletproof SUVs on the ready in the gated compound, with phone calls from ambassadors of the US and UK urging the party not to venture outside, with offers from businessmen asking for permission to fly in firebrand leaders of the Lawyers' Movement, with party members on the expected route asking for directions, with family matriarchs scooting around with holy threads and talismanic scriptures and with eyes glued to the one TV in the room, one thing was becoming clear to Nawaz Sharif. He was now the person everyone was calling.

The movement that had begun in the house of an unlikely chief justice and had then raged on the streets for two years was now sitting with him in his drawing room in Model Town. When he got into his SUV and cameras showed the bulletproof vehicle leaving his compound, police chiefs changed alliances. They stopped their platoons from firing. In another six hours, the movement had in fact won and the chief justice with the moustache was restored.

After the restoration, we discovered that the chief justice with the moustache was as flawed a man as any. In the end, the movement, like all true movements, was not about the man in front of it but about the idea behind it—that no man is above the law.

V
TRUST ME

Ten Days of School

Hyder, when you were in third grade, during your summer vacations, I returned home one day from Islamabad and you asked me where I had been. I had been to meet the Atomic Energy Commission. So I explained to you that I had spent the last few days helping some scientists who made nuclear bombs. I was impressed that you reprimanded me for dealing with people who were busy making bombs for killing Indians. I was thus forbidden by you from meeting such evil people. I was impressed that you could form your opinions at such an age and that somehow I was able to sneak some contrarian thinking into your head between the Nintendo and the Game Boy.

But this soon changed, dramatically.

Your summer vacations ended a fortnight later. School started. Ten days into your term, you came straight from school and before removing your uniform, hunted me down, and demanded, 'I need a bazooka.'

'Why?' I asked.

'To kill Indians,' you said. 'They have conspired with Satan to make five hundred statues and Allah will be pleased if we help Him,' you explained.

'Ten days,' I thought, 'only ten.'

Such is the impact of school. Children take school very seriously. And these years decide what the nation ultimately deems important.

I am not worried about you. I am sure you will, in time, come around. But I am concerned when I multiply this thought with the number of schools and the number of teachers and the number of students out there. How will we all come around and think the way the rest of the world thinks.

∞

Schools. They will break us. Or make us. Not madrassas. Madrassas affect only one per cent of Pakistan's total population. It is the government-run school system that is breeding what it should be cleansing.

A recent study in Pakistan showed that educated people were more accepting of suicide bombings and of al-Qaeda and the Taliban than illiterate people.[*] This for me was one indicator of the side effect of education in Pakistan. In other words, the unfortunate souls who have not had the luxury of education still hold common-sense views their mothers taught them, but the fortunate ones have been infected by a lowly paid bureaucrat's estimation of what it means to be a Pakistani. How can I explain to you that my father was a Muslim and so was his father before him. But neither had been taught Islamiyat in school. They got away with thinking that Khuda was Allah and Allah was Khuda. They

---

[*]Pew Research 2009

thought it uncouth for a young man to support a beard. They sang songs and danced with abandon. They were schooled in small towns and villages and yet were able to read and write in English, Urdu and Punjabi. They were proud of who they were.

They were not without prejudice as you and I are not without prejudice, for prejudice is a very human failing. But the schools they went to understood this and tried to wash away prejudice through textbooks—not heighten it.

We live in an interconnected world where the concept of national boundaries is becoming more and more inconsequential. The people who succeed will have built the most bridges across national boundaries—networks of commerce, of scientific collaboration, of trust.

In this new world, prejudice of others will reduce networks, not increase them. Prejudice will thus reduce our productivity. If we have to win, we must become friendly. To become friendly, we must change our textbooks.

Lessons from the War

Explosions and attacks are filed in myriad compartments by us all. My friends in Punjab and in Karachi keep blaming the Americans for everything.

'It is all a big conspiracy,' they say.

In the meantime, unbeknownst to my friends, the Pashtun keep blaming Punjabis and the Pakistan Army for foisting the Taliban upon them.

'It is all a big conspiracy,' they say.

The truth is dead.

This is war.

Listen.

The first casualty of war is the truth. It is this demise of truth that has led me to believe that we are in fact at war.

∽

'War is good business,' an Azerbaijani officer once told me when his country was at war with Georgia and he had offered me a ride on his jeep. He sported Ray-Ban aviators and smoked smuggled cigarettes and was the only Azerbaijani who held his head high, who smiled and whose uniform was spotless. When I asked him what he did in the army, Commander Mehmaan smiled broadly, and explained simply. 'I make dollars,' he said.

∽

I was standing in a village in Italy in 2007 when I got the news that my father-in-law had been kidnapped. I rushed back to Pakistan.

Thirty days later, the episode ended over a meal in a tent in another village...in FATA.

Our party counted out the money. The atmosphere was more cordial than most business meetings. We were given a phone to talk to my father-in-law to ascertain that we were talking to the correct hostage. 'If we release the wrong doctor, you have to pay again to release the correct doctor. You better make sure you are talking to "your" doctor,' emphasized the chief of the *lashkar*. And then, while 'our' doctor got his release and was transported from a third location back to his hospital, our party was feted with lamb and nuts and tea and, for entertainment, treated to recordings of the actions of the lashkar against the Pakistan Army. Recordings of beheadings of Pakistani soldiers were interrupted for prayer breaks and then restarted.

The one ex-soldier in our party, an officer retired from a premier intelligence agency[*]—who was the guarantor of this deal and the reason everyone was so relaxed—averted

---

[*] I have been advised by friends not to use the name of this intelligence agency. Instead to refer to it as it is referred to in most newspaper reports.

his eyes politely. Six months earlier, he had been serving in the military and it had been his job to befriend these lashkars up and down the FATA. It seemed that he had done his job well. Of course, friendship has a price. We had paid it in advance.

After two hours, Doctor Saab arrived back at his hospital and the drama ended with bear hugs in the tent and with such heartfelt joy that some in our party left the scene with respect for the kidnappers and for their strict adherence to Islam.

If I ever get kidnapped, reread this chapter carefully and follow my instructions.

First, trust the kidnapper. He will be a professional. He will know his business better than you. He will have done due diligence on you and on me before striking. And he will lead you gently, though frustratingly slow, in the right direction.

Second, go to Sakhakot. Sakhakot is a small truck stop just outside the limits of Swat police, on the border of the provincially administered tribal area in Malakand. The first call we received from the kidnappers, even before I arrived on the scene, was that we should go to Sakhakot. We never went there because we thought it was a trap. Who would we meet there? What will we do there? How would we know what to do when we got there? 'Go to Sakhakot,' was all they said and we never went.

Your Nana was not the only person, Hyder, who was kidnapped from Wah in those days. Other families were going through the same drama spread all over town. None of us shared our strategies during the kidnappings, but we compared notes when the ordeal was over.

I discovered one family that agreed to this first request from the kidnappers and straight away went to Sakhakot. There they discovered a few chai khanas and hotels, a single roadside grocery shop stocked with cooking cylinders and cans of ghee. They randomly parked the car and waited nervously. Soon, a broker—more real estate agent than bootlegger—leaned into their window and asked, 'What was lifted?' Before anyone could answer, he clarified, 'Man or machine, we will find it inshallah,' putting his customers at rest. Here was a man who specialized in putting deals together. You will find many of them in Sakhakot. They will negotiate a rate with you, between ten to thirty thousand rupees. This rate, once negotiated, will buy you his headhunting services. He will get details of the kidnapping from you, date, place, description of the person. Then he will ask you to wait in a hotel while he makes some phone calls. In a few hours he will locate the true kidnapper and put you in touch with him. The kidnapper will then negotiate a price, between one and three lakhs, and you can be home the next day.

This worked for the people who took the plunge. They paid the lowest amounts and got their man in the least time. So, go to Sakhakot.

Third, if you miss the bus to Sakhakot, remember that the kidnapper will call you at irregular intervals, about two times a week, but he will already have hinted his final price in his first demand. The consensus is that he will always ask ten times more than he expects you to pay. If he starts his negotiations from two hundred lakhs he means to close the deal at twenty—based on his assessment of your assets and income. It is important to quickly arrive close to the closing number and then stick to it.

It is important also to remember that the person on the phone would only be a paid employee. He will, at any given time, be handling about a dozen negotiations for a salary of about twenty thousand per month. He will have his own car—probably a white Corolla—and multiple phones with multiple SIMs, all in that car. He will not have met any of the kidnapped persons and he will not have any idea where the kidnapped persons are being held. He will have only enough information to allow him to hold negotiations. He will, on a given day, start his working day from Swat, make a phone call to one family, note down the results, move on to Mardan, then, from another phone with a separate SIM, make another call to a different family. He will continue these calls all the way up to Peshawar, where he will rest for the night and then begin the next day—on the road again. He will make sure that he does not mix up the phones and also that the phones are switched off when not being used. He will also have a phone of his own and will use it only for communications to his internal supply chain to relay results of negotiations, to note any additional information gleaned from the kidnapped person that he may need to strengthen his negotiating position in the discussions. He will be stressed and under pressure to close. But he will, when he gets near to his target price, have to transfer the deal to his boss, who will then call you directly from a different location and a different phone.

This is when you and the kidnapper will finally talk and

this is when you will be faced with your biggest decision—after missing the first bus to Sakhakot.

Once the amount is agreed upon, you will have to agree on the way that this amount will be transferred and the kidnapped person released. How will you trust a known criminal to not go back on his word? How will you know that he will not take the money and shoot you as well?

My fourth advice is to then take the plunge. The kidnapper has a reputation to protect. His business does not end with you only. He has other deals to close as well. If word gets out that he does not keep his promises, his entire supply chain will break down. He will keep his word. And he will make sure he protects you, and his money.

I talked to one such family that took the plunge. The person who was kidnapped owned a petrol station and was kidnapped from his station almost at the same time as your Nana. His eldest son broke all contact with the police and the rest of the world, and ensconced himself in his bedroom with a phone and a charger—coming out only to eat. He negotiated rapidly with the kidnapper, reached a deal, told a close friend to withdraw money from a bank, and with that trusted friend, got into a car and started driving towards Peshawar with a phone on the ready.

They got instructions to reach Nowshera. Then, before they got to Nowshera, they were told to stop next to a Fanta billboard. They were told to simply drop the bag of money beside the billboard and drive on. They did so. A little later, they got a call that the money was received and counted. Their father would now be released. A couple of hours later, the father reached home. They paid ten lakhs.

Their ordeal lasted ten days.

After Sakhakot, this was the second most successful strategy. Negotiate quickly, involve as few people as possible, and take the plunge when asked.

Just as the negotiator is only a paid employee working at arm's length from the rest of the organization, another key position in the kidnapping enterprise is that of the safe house manager. He is responsible for keeping all hostages healthy, secure and incommunicado. Like the negotiator, he only knows as much as he needs to know.

According to Doctor Saab, he was kept in an urban villa not far from where he was kidnapped. The villa's windows had been bricked up but otherwise it was a normal middle-class villa that had a typical lounge and dining room with kitchen on the ground floor. Three bedrooms were on the first floor and one on the ground. Doctor Saab was accommodated in the bedroom on the ground floor and three other hostages upstairs. A posse of guards occupied the lounge and watched television all day and most of the night. The residents of the bedrooms were also brought out to the lounge in rotation for a bit of fresh air but never together, so they could not meet each other. A cleaning lady came in the morning to clean all the rooms and a cook was available to make special meals if required.

The safe house manager, barely thirty years old, used to come in after lunch and stay until midnight. He had some trouble with his kidneys and would spend many hours with Doctor Saab discussing the benefits of watermelons and green tea. He discussed his business plans. He explained that business was good. He was running at full capacity.

He was trying to decide whether to invest in a larger safe house or possibly buy out his neighbour.

Then, one day, while they were thus sitting and discussing property rates, the safe house manager got a phone call. He said it was from his contact in the premier intelligence agency. He was warning that a police raid was imminent. He then asked Doctor Saab not to panic. It would all be over soon. Doctor Saab was told to stay inside his room and not to make noise. After a half hour of tense wait, police sirens wailed in the distance, getting nearer and nearer. Very soon blue and red flashing lights started jangling through the cracks in the doorways and boarded up skylights. Then, the main door was opened with a crash. Multiple heavy boots entered the villa and tramped heavily upstairs only to tramp back, equally heavily, downstairs. The sirens then blared again and the posse left the locale as noisily as it had entered. The front door then shut again, gently, deliberately.

The safe house manager popped his head into Doctor Saab's bedroom, gave the all clear sign and popped out again.

So, my fifth piece of advice is to break contact with the police.

The police, as soon as you file a report, gets to tap your landline phone. If you discuss deposits and withdrawals and drop-off points on your landline, they will find out. And they will be very interested in any car with a large amount of cash moving alone in the evening in their circle of influence. Word that a shadowy payment is going to be made could easily reach the ears of other criminals.

The police have senior IT specialists in Rawalpindi who

parse through phone bills and try to connect phone calls and phone sets. These IT specialists are understaffed considering the number of phones and SIMs and kidnappings, but they have made some spectacular catches in the past years. They work in isolation from local police stations because they do not trust local police.

Our premier intelligence agency goes one step further. They can intercept live calls, both landline and mobile. They make recordings and can compare voices with those in their database. Their operation is more sophisticated than the police's, but even more removed from the local station. There is absolutely no way for local police to access this database that the premier intelligence agency guards so possessively. Contact with the premier intelligence agency has to be made by the bereaved family using friends and contacts.

When you try hard enough you too will discover these capabilities and you, too, will find friends and contacts who will lead you to these discoveries. Remember, though, that the kidnapping enterprise will already know of these capabilities as a matter of routine market analysis. Only the most desperate and incompetent kidnapper will nowadays use phones and SIMs without taking simple precautions. Any organized kidnapping enterprise worth its name has by now infiltrated the intelligence agencies. To achieve their aims, intelligence agencies must keep in touch with criminal organizations, what the army calls unsavoury characters. Remember too that such contact can never always be one way. Information leaks. Small, petty information that the premier intelligence agency is not worried about safeguarding as a national security issue is bartered and sold in petty discussions without any pain to the organization's larger charter. But it can be very valuable to criminals and can mean life or death for someone caught on the wrong side of it.

So, my sixth piece of advice is to stay away from official contact with the premier intelligence agency.

We did not follow any of this advice ourselves, of course.

By the time I arrived from Italy, the Sakhakot overture had been dismissed, the head of the provincial police had been contacted, the operational head of the premier intelligence agency for this area had been notified and the local press was running a ticker tape message of the kidnapping on cable channels.

As a result, the local police SHO was most cooperative in that he would drop in every couple of days to break bread with us and explain that the police had just sacrificed a black goat to ward off the evil shadow.

In a week's time, things settled into a pattern. Doctor Saab's house was manned by four of us—myself, two of Doctor Saab's sons who were doctors in England, and a nephew from Sargodha. We spent the next month indoors nearly all the time, next to a couple of phones, negotiating not with the kidnapper but with ourselves.

Then the phone would ring and the Pathan accent of the kidnapper's assistant would fall on our ears like blessings from Allah. Sometimes he would plead, sometimes he would berate and sometimes he would even pray for our shared ordeal to quickly be over. All the time, though, I now know, he was guiding us forward. He continued telling us to break contact with the police and the premier intelligence agency.

We did break contact with the police but continued working with the premier intelligence agency's phone system—until, one day, the kidnapper's assistant told us something that was known only to the premier intelligence agency. The premier intelligence agency was leaking information to the kidnappers and now, even if we wanted, we could not break off contact with it. They were tracking all our phones. The kidnappers knew what we were doing. They were concerned but not worried. They had done all of this before.

Finally we arrived at a settlement. Sixty lakhs for Doctor Saab and his car, and we were able to talk to the kidnapper directly. But there was a problem. Because we had continued contact with the premier intelligence agency, the kidnappers could no longer trust us. They felt insecure. While they had Doctor Saab, they held the cards, but once the deal was done they would no longer be in charge. How could they trust us to quietly disappear back into our normal routine, to leave them be? They needed a guarantee.

We needed to find a guarantor.

The deal was final, the agreement was done, but like two cross-border companies transacting business across an ocean, we needed to find a credible bank that would open a letter of credit guaranteeing compliance from both sides.

'How can we find a guarantor who knows you and us?' we asked him.

'You will find him, trust me, you will,' he said, and put down the phone.

We tracked down an upstart member of the provincial

assembly from Swat who almost too readily agreed to play the role of guarantor. In our next phone call, we transmitted his name to the kidnapper. In two days he called back that his due diligence on the MPA did not give the confidence to proceed. The MPA was asking for too much money for his services. We needed to try again, he said encouragingly.

At this point, Doctor Saab's nephew whispered an idea. 'What about Major Nasir?' His friend Major Nasir was an officer recently retired from the premier intelligence agency. So we met him.

Here is my final piece of advice. If you mess up on any of the previous six instructions, go to Major Nasir.

Major Nasir was of the same age as me and had retired only six months ago from active service in the premier intelligence agency in South Waziristan. He had a nice villa in Islamabad with two cars in the driveway and a farm. It took him a day to make contact with the kidnappers. The kidnappers readily accepted him as the guarantor. He asked for fifteen lakhs to give to his friends who were helping him. Now we were in his hands.

Two days later, I drove a car with us and Major Nasir to Peshawar. Sixty lakh rupees were stuffed into a tissue paper box and kept on the dashboard. Major Nasir took us to a posh locality where we met a young man who was a previous client of Major Nasir's. His father, he said, had been kidnapped from his factory in Hazara. He then walked us around his neighbourhood, which seemed eerily deserted. Each house we passed had had a kidnapping. 'The father here, came back after two months. The son here, still not back. This one was back within one day,' he casually explained. We waited until dark. We waited into the morning. No one talked about why we were there or the sixty lakhs sitting in a tissue box on the dashboard. I kept the car key as close as possible.

Then Major Nasir entered in a rush with some Peshawari caps in his hand, grumbling into the phone about trousers and jeans and T-shirts, but got us into the car again and we began to drive. He did not tell us where we were going or whom we were meeting. The only negotiation taking place was on the dress code. It seemed, in the area we were about to enter, the fine for not wearing a cap was five hundred rupees and jeans were simply out of the question. But this was not an insurmountable problem for Major Nasir, who wanted to make sure there was no diplomatic issue on the way. He did his job well. In only five minutes, we began following a Toyota 4x4 and a Toyota 4x4 began following us. We drove in silence until we began seeing men with Sten guns manning the sides of the road at regular intervals, letting us pass without bother, until we arrived at a camp.

While the money was being counted and we munched on pistachio nuts, the head of the lashkar requested with clear eyes and a soft voice that we must all promise never to scorn him in our prayers because all that had transpired was the will of Allah and he was but an instrument. He explained that divine punishment for Doctor Saab, for some sin to which only Allah is privy, was being administered through his hands. He himself had prayed to Allah that Doctor Saab's sins should be forgiven and our common prayers had resulted in Doctor Saab's release. Neither he, nor any of his men, felt even a hint of guilt. They went about their work carefully and professionally.

To this day, I have no idea where this camp was or what was the name of the man we met.

But I know the name of the business he was running. Some call it war, others call it jihad, but it is good business.

Under a Darkened Moon

'A mosque. In America.' I said slowly.

'A mosque. In America.' Hamid Pia gave a wry smile.

We strolled through his leafy American town. His wife was putting his kids to sleep and we could now talk.

'Awkward?'

'Awkward.'

After 9/11, briefly, Hamid Pia had to be more American than the Americans. He had to paste the American flag on his door and in his car, just in case. Some years had passed since that fateful Tuesday.

'You see, my new mosque is quite a scandal...for my Muslim brothers.' Hamid Pia smiled his wry smile again. We quietly enjoyed the irony. '*They* say it is not a mosque, not where kids run around and women cook chawal and girls and boys eat together. *They* do not approve.'

Both of us smiled and walked knowing how improbable each step was, how fantastic that we both could share a walk here after so much had passed. Our hands were cosy in our pockets.

'I know who *they* are.' I said.

'I know too.' Hamid Pia was not surprised. A bit tired of the subject but not surprised. We had separately searched long and hard to find out. We had both seen the leaves turn colour, but we had not talked for a decade. We had both seen separately how slowly Khuda had become Allah, Punjabi dupattas were replaced by Arabic abayas, Ramzan had become Ramadan.

'The Saudis are afraid of the Shia.' Hamid Pia exhaled, if only to keep the conversation going.

'But Hamid Pia, we were not Shia. Why would the Saudi convert the converted?'

'We were dangerously Shia. Look at us from the outside. From the outside, we appeared a closet Shia people. We have had two uncontested popular leaders. Both were Shia. Persian was our state language before English. We have many native Persian speakers, our old monuments have Persian verses carved on them and we are on the border of Iran. To the Saudis, we were dangerously Shia.'

The Shia are on one edge of the Islamic thought spectrum. Our schoolbook Islamiyat and Saudi Islam are on the opposite edge. This spectrum is not discussed in polite conversation because schoolbook Islamiyat tells us that there is no spectrum, no difference in opinion, that there is but one Islam, one that ideally ties all of us together.

Before Islamiyat, our nation had resided in a zone pretty much in the centre of this broad spectrum. Now, after thirty years of studying this kind of Islamiyat, we were bound to have swung towards this, the Saudi edge.

Hamid Pia's thesis was correct but not complete. The Saudi were afraid not just of the Shia on the opposite edge of the spectrum but those in the middle ground as well. And Hamid Pia in his youth had represented that middle ground.

'Hamid Pia, the biggest challenge to Saudi thought comes from within Saudi Arabia itself. The Saud tribe conquered Mecca and Medina, the land you revere as the Hejaz, by force. The Saudi is not a Hejazi. But the Prophet, his family and his followers were all Hejazis. When the Hejazis venerate, like you, the Prophet and his family and their followers, the Saudis become insecure. That insecurity is the reason you were weaned away from your divine veneration of the Prophet and his family. Your love had consequences. Political consequences.'

I waited for my thesis to sink in. For Hamid Pia, this was a sad thesis that he had no energy to discuss. But he understood me perfectly, as we could—since we were boys—understand each other's every grimace, every joke.

We swung onto another road as the moon slunk behind a cloud. An elm vied with an oak to block the lonesome yellow of the street lamps, all in a row. We were wading into darkness. Hamid Pia surveyed the expanse of my thesis, which I needed him to vet. He matched it against a lifetime of reproach. He slowly imagined how his own love for the Prophet had made distant kings tremble. A flicker of sadness crossed his brow as he thought how he had to bury his love for the Prophet into the deeper recesses of his mien only because the rulers of the most glorious throne on earth were insecure. And he felt a curious sobbing in his heart for his Prophet, whose land was under occupation. This enveloped him in silence.

We walked steadily in the dark.

Hamid Pia's tall frame had filled out in America and now, as he walked in his shalwar kameez, slowly and deliberately, his silhouette was almost regal. I walked in Bermuda shorts and the regular slap of my flip-flops was the only noise that broke the eerie silence.

We were silent because we knew what the other was thinking. We had allowed an upstart kingdom to change our beliefs. We had learnt to be ashamed of our amazingly passionate nature. And we had been dragged into some other kingdom's war. Instead of exporting our tolerance, we had instead imported someone else's insecurity.

Thus, the politics of the Middle East, the tantalizing struggle for control of the most important throne on earth, results in confusion and death on the streets of our country.

It is up to us to divorce ourselves from this struggle by remembering that political struggle is different from religious struggle. Democracy has given us a way to settle political differences. This way is not available to Middle Eastern monarchies. We can, even now, settle our political differences.

And religious differences? Religious differences need not be resolved.

It is good for religious differences to persist, to give more choices to young people like you to choose freely from, in a system that does not give preference to any one religious thought, in a system that lets the best idea prevail in a free market for religious thought, in a system that divorces religion from the invisible hands of government, a system that will transform us from the battleground of Islam into a bridge where the Persian and the Arab will freely come to transact business and learn democracy. Our simultaneous love for both Mecca and Tabriz will no longer be a bad thing.

We walked thus without words, our steps following a common rhythm, when we saw two black men rounding a corner.

They were muscular and walked deliberately towards us. We kept walking. They crossed the street and we noticed, at the pace we were walking, that our paths would coincide when they cross the road. Hamid Pia and I did not need to talk. We instinctively knew we could not show any fear. Both of us straightened up to our maximum heights and made sure our strides did not falter. The two black men too walked without breaking their strides and our paths suddenly coincided and they began to walk only a step ahead of us and we walked steadily behind them. Thus, we walked, in eerie silence, the four of us, in lock step under a darkened moon at midnight in New Jersey, my flip-flops the only sound now for miles. We had walked half a block like this when the two black men stopped us.

'Hey man, we can't take this any longer, man!' the first one cried in exasperation.

'It's like Freddy Krueger, man. This place and these flip-flops, man!' The other threw up his hands.

'What do you want?' the first one interjected.

'We ain't got nothin' on us man, promise!' the other said.

A Pious Bureaucrat

A PATWARI is the first building block of bureaucracy, the keeper of land records of the smallest land revenue unit. All sales and records of rural tenancy are penned by his hand. He is also the junior-most government servant and earns a salary four grades lower than that of the junior-most school teacher.

I once found myself in Gujranwala in the drawing room of a man who used to wind the coils that go into the motors of the fans made in the city. Here, while I waited for lunch to be served, I found myself seated next to a nice young man who was explaining to me his career path, that he had been selected by the government to become a patwari and that nowadays he was attending patwar classes in Lala Musa—only an hour away. He explained, for no apparent reason, that boys from very good families were attending these classes with him. To press the point home, he elaborated that he normally gets a lift to school from one of his classmates who has his own Corolla 2D and who also keeps a Kalashnikov next to the driver's seat.

He did not fully notice but I felt an ever so slight tightening of the sphincter.

'Why,' I asked, with a masterly air of disinterest,

'would a man with a 2D and a Kalashnikov want to be a patwari?'

'My friend does not want to be a patwari. He wants to go to America, but his father does not agree. His father is a patwari himself and employs a number of ex-patwaris under him. He has asked his son to clear the patwar course and then he would run the son's patwar also, and the son can go to America.'

I was at that point a Yale graduate, the son of a high court judge, the grandson of a top eye surgeon and at least a decade of work away from being able to buy a 2D. Something was amiss.

I am not the first person to notice that something has been amiss in the land of the pure for some time now. But we all believe as a matter of faith, that the solution to this problem, as to all other problems, is the implementation of sharia. No one can be corrupt under sharia, we believe. You too will believe this when you come out of school. But let us put this belief to the test.

A patwari's function is to read records, write records and retrieve records from large canvas maps and onerous paper ledgers. He is paid a fee for providing this service. The market decides that the fee it is willing to pay for this service is well above the salary the patwari can draw. Therefore the market steps in and provides the difference because the market must function. Lands need to be rented, mortgaged, sold. The market cannot wait for the salary of the data keeper to keep pace with its need. The market will pay a fee to anyone who can provide the service.

It would gladly pay the government, were the government

only to ask—but a government run by government servants will never ask.

Only a government of representatives, of people who use government's services, can think about moving this fee from the patwari and routing it into government revenue. If we are going to pay the patwari less and the revenue department more, the revenue department will need to devise a system that reduces the importance of the patwari in the record-keeping mechanism.

You have already learnt in your computer class, Hyder, that a computer's basic job is to read, write and retrieve records. You can understand that a patwari basically does the exact same thing as a computer. Day after day. A computer can very easily replace him.

Since the 1980s, a World Bank grant has been paying the Pakistan government to run a pilot project in the Punjab district of Kasur to computerize land records. This project has been running at a snail's pace because government servants have been in charge. For twenty-five years, nothing. Then a subtle change. Democracy began to reassert its control over government servants. And within five years this project was rescaled, indigenized and implemented in three large divisions of Punjab. A democratic government must retrieve power from government servants (patwaris) and extract the most benefits from government services for ordinary people. Wherever these computers have taken over the work of patwaris, land records are being retrieved via the Internet and corruption has been minimized. Faster, more transparent land transactions mean that more bottlenecked capital can now be brought into use. Corruption has declined—dramatically.

Now, let us look at our original, desperate schoolboy premise—that all solutions are written into the sharia. Here, we found the solution was democracy and computers. Both are within our reach.

Think. Do not jump.

Once, as a young man, I stood in a balcony of a hospital on Jail Road, chatting with a banker, whiling away time, impressed with the banker's ability to spin pieces of very engaging conversation out of almost any clue presented to him. As we paced to the end of the balcony we could see the rooftop of the Shadman Police Station beneath us. The police station suddenly and smoothly wove its way into our conversation.

'The SHO of the Shadman Police Station is a very good friend of mine,' he said. 'Very helpful. A good boy. Cultured, not like police officers at all,' he recalled. 'One really finds out the mettle of a person in times of crisis. You know, my car was stolen...'

'How?' I interjected. The banker was almost taken aback.

'Well, it was complicated, you see.'

'Where were you?'

'I was in the car.'

'When it was stolen?'

'Yes, didn't you know? Anyway, I called the SHO and he arranged everything and that is how I got to really know him. Wonderful fellow, very sophisticated. Not like other policemen at all. He is cultured and has refined tastes. He loves football. In fact, he was at the Italian embassy just a day ago to get his visa. You see, he always watches the World Cup Final and the UEFA Cup Final live in the stadium. He just loves football.'

Again that faint tightening of the sphincter, but it went away.

An SHO is a station house officer. Like a patwari, he is the basic building block of police bureaucracy. An SHO normally works at all times of the day, knows all the miscreants, drug dealers, encroachers, beggars, bootleggers, kidnappers and prayer leaders on his beat. He is able to translate this knowledge, if he is clever, into a very lucrative service that can include protection, recovery of stolen goods or people, dispute arbitration, asset repossession and loan recovery.

People are willing to pay handsomely for these services, but the supply and demand in this marketplace is such that the ordinary person finds himself priced out of the market. Police services are therefore only affordable for the affluent or the powerful.

The poor find themselves on the receiving end of torture and incarceration that is the currency in which this market measures performance. But the poor too must find ways to survive. So they too have adapted. They have found protection in the private sector. The private sector has developed products that can be bought by the poor—not at the going retail price—but through a membership in a number of protection clubs. These are called mafias in Italy, militant groups in FATA, tehriks in Karachi, and lashkars in Punjab. One family member's membership in a lashkar gives other family members immunity from police torture and undue incarceration. Today these lashkars have become more powerful than the police and the police force has lost its monopoly position in its market. For the poor end-user, this is not as bad as it sounds. With the demise of the monopoly of police, he is able to get market-friendly prices for police-like services with multiple lashkars competing hard for his business. These lashkars are more efficient and allow the user to buy the level of service that he or she wishes to buy, with just one caveat. In this free-market system, the criminal too is able to buy services freely. He may need to pay a premium but he can nevertheless buy.

This is the caveat that hurts. It is this caveat we see when we catch a Shia complaining that the bomber of his congregation roams the streets free. It is this caveat that forces people to pine for those mythical times we have all read about in our textbooks when sharia was in force and peace reigned above all.

I ask you not to jump to emotional conclusions but to just peel back the layers of complication I have just described. You will slowly arrive at the realization that the fix to our police system is to be discovered not in mythical times of yore but in modern policing systems perfected by normal modern countries. We can look at Switzerland or Singapore or Malaysia, even at India, and we will discover that our police system lacks something very basic: local oversight. We only need to make sure that the SHO is answerable not to his boss in a distant district headquarters but to the residents of the local area he polices.

This simple and, in fact, not revolutionary change would nonetheless revolutionize policing and strike at the heart of the business model of lashkars. It will force the SHO to regain his monopoly in his marketplace.

One can, similarly, break down every problem slowly into its basic components and discover that government is just the sum of a collection of services that the market cannot fairly provide. These services need to be provided by government servants but overseen by elected representatives. That is all there is to it.

Government seems very sexy to us when we frame it in kings and caliphs who parley justice under God's shadow. Government then begins to appear sacred. Now, if we frame it in very mundane terms, such as bus timetables and budget overruns and sewage sludge and traffic congestion and revenue receipts and tax, we discover that government is a very worldly exercise, capable of being managed by imperfect humans without any larger divine design. It is this realization that cannot today be mentioned openly.

This realization is called secularism.

Secularism is a dirty word in Pakistan. Many a scholar blanches on stage when confronted with it because we have been taught in schools that Islam is a way of life. It cannot therefore be separated from any part of life, least of all from government.

I too had believed this for the better part of my life. It has taken me many years of introspection despite overwhelming evidence to get myself to question this fundamental belief. I have now discovered many instances of secularism within Islam. For instance, no one told us that the Bengalis, as soon as they separated from Pakistan, quickly adopted a secular constitution that confidently declared that nation with more Muslims than Pakistan to be a country with no state religion, a country run according to man-made law.

Turkey is the most powerful Muslim economic power today. It, too, is secular. It is being run by an Islamist party, but the constitution and the government have no religion. In fact, Erdogan, the three-time elected Islamist prime minister of Turkey, whose influence over right-wing parties reaches from Algeria all the way to Pakistan, is very clear in his thoughts that government must remain neutral to religion. When he went to Tahrir Square in support of the Muslim Brotherhood's resurgence in Egyptian politics, he made it a point to communicate to the Egyptians that as much as he supports religious parties within Egypt, he firmly believes that Egypt should be secular. This statement by Erdogan has never been publicized here in the land of the pure. It did appear in the West, along with his photograph on the cover of *TIME* magazine.

Secularism is not the only way discovered for humans to form a dignified society, it is also one of the messages we learn from Islamic history itself. The success of early Islam too was in its embrace of secularism.

Medina was the first secular state. The Pact of Medina, the first written constitution of a state, was secular. It had no mention of a state religion, nor of law of man being subservient to the laws of God. It allowed for different Jewish and Christian tribes to continue their practices as before and allowed for government to stay out of religion. And it was written about fourteen hundred years ago.

In fact, you will be shocked, as was I, that the ummah referred to in the Pact of Medina very explicitly included Jews, Christians and all other non-Muslim signatories to the document. The ummah, for that document, was everyone agreeing to the pact, not everyone agreeing to the Kalima.

What I tell you is so far removed from what you would otherwise hear that you will find it difficult to believe me. But this is a penny that will eventually drop. And this is the future you will eventually arrive at. The faster you get there the better.

A Reason to Be

The year was 2009. The world had just entered the great recession. We had just got back to democracy. Elections in the frontier province had just been swept by a party with a red flag and a communistic manifesto. Swat, a district of this province, had been taken over by Talibanized militants. Malala Yousafzai's blog had started appearing at BBC.com under a pseudonym and secular minds who had just demonstrated their majority in the polls were being swept from the valley.

Then, with two hours' notice, the army had announced that it was attacking the militants. In a day, an exodus of Swati civilians had clogged the fields of Mardan. A UNHCR* camp designed for Afghan refugees of the last war was now ready to take Swatis.

I was following the situation with the help of Swati dissidents, aka Indian agents. The news thus reached me faster than it did others in the plains. I called Sajjad, the son of a soldier who had died fighting the Indians in 1971, my comrade in such situations, and both of us left for Mardan in the middle of the Lahore night, with all the cash we had

---

*United Nations High Commission for Refugees

at home, and little else. In Mardan we split up.

Thus it was that I suddenly found myself in the Jalozai refugee camp, surrounded by tents as far as I could see. The fertile watered fields of the Malakand valley were witnessing a strange dust bowl contest for food, shelter and privacy. Families were arriving by the truckload. On arrival, they were given water and juice by jihadi organizations from Punjab. But then the system got confusing. How does one get a space, a tent, a meal? Each family had to figure this out on its own. I saw a line of men that started out as a line but then became a melee close to an open window of a UN van. This van was the bottleneck. Each family had to be registered there. A lone UN worker with a laptop sat inside it, entered the data for each family, and issued a Refugee Registration card. This enabled the card holder to receive a tent, a space in the camp, a bucket, plates and dry ration. The card also allowed holders to fill their plates from the field kitchen, which cooked three large meals a day. Getting to the kitchen contractor's ladle three times a day, though, required gargantuan effort for a family not used to elbowing through a throng of hungry refugees.

The men who explained the system to me were shopkeepers and bank clerks and school administrators whose families were unable to eat because they could not get to the front of the line for the cards or if they had cards, could not get to the contractor's ladle over the shoulders of others. Labourers and peasants were more used to scrambling for their rights and so they were faring much better in this reversed environment. I saw growing panic and grown men twice my size crying in desperation.

I discovered that all the organs of state were present in the camp and that they were doing a fantastic job in such a hopeless situation. But there was one thing missing. The organs of the state were treating these people as the people of another country. Like refugees from Afghanistan. Although, these refugees were locals and had locally elected representatives. But those representatives were missing.

In their stead, government servants were in charge. But government servants should not be in charge.

The problem was actually not that difficult. Very quickly, standing in a torn kurta and plastic slippers in a dusty clearance, I started taking decisions that people started to implement. The first thing I 'ordered' was an election. I asked the men talking to me to get the heads of each tent together and then to elect by show of hands a governing council and its chairman. That governing council, I declared, would then negotiate the way forward with the camp organizers. I then went to the police contingent standing to one side and 'ordered' them to make sure the line to the UN van was not broken. Two disinterested policemen with sticks, thinking I was some government personage, quickly managed this simple task.

Then, with a glass of water thrust into my face, I began to compute the time it took the person in the UN van to enter data. I had made a living from data entry in another life. I assumed that the UN would have a standard data entry interface and even an idiot would be able to fill it in if he only had access. They needed more laptops here. Even one more laptop would double the speed of entry. Two would triple the flow. I then spied, in the midst of another crowd, an African face with the air of experience about him. I quickly got to him and he turned out to be the head of the UNHCR in Pakistan. I asked him why we could not have more laptops here. He said he most certainly could arrange it but, pointing to another imperious and weighty man, I had to first talk to the commissioner. The commissioner was a Pathan with walrus moustaches and a starched, light blue, slightly scented kurta. Without a moment's pause, I turned to him. He was already eyeing my incongruous figure from his experienced blue eyes but still had to ask me who I was. 'Where are you from?' he asked, the catch-all question necessary to judging one's adversary before engaging.

'I am from the Punjab,' I said. 'I represent some donors who are extremely perturbed.' And then I asked him for the laptops.

'Son,' he began with an expansive hand, 'I must look at the bigger picture. I am responsible for these people. I cannot spend time looking for one laptop.' He sneered. Then he gestured to three men who stood in identical Nehru jackets in descending order. 'Look, this is the district commissioner, this is the assistant commissioner, this is the tehsildar,' he said. Somehow this sealed his argument. He wanted me to understand that he was the head of all government servants in this district. There was no room for discussion. The battle was lost.

The UNHCR's head then stood aside and advised me. Allocations will be made in Peshawar, he said. It could be done, but in Peshawar. So I returned to my now very loyal constituency. I asked whether anyone had a number of their representative. The Swatis then huddled and finally someone was able to find on his phone a cell number of their recently elected representative to the provincial assembly. As I called it, my brain, buoyed by the support around me, suddenly became very clear.

Carefully, without showing any anger or dismay, I explained to the other side of the line that I was in Jalozai camp in a sea of his constituents. It was like being in a shop run by the servants. And the master of the shop was nowhere to be seen. He was the master, I assured him, not the government servants who appeared to be in charge. The poor man had no idea who I was. I berated him for having left his people without a leader in this time of need. He then apologized, explaining that he was in Peshawar trying the best he could in pushing the government for help. He was, in fact, about to enter a committee meeting with secretaries (senior government servants) to discuss the crisis in Swat.

'Good.' I said. 'Then let us work together.' I asked him to get more UNHCR laptops allocated for the camp. Then I explained that the Jalozai camp was electing its own council, that government servants needed to run the camp but only with the advice of this council. I had no idea what kind of man was on the other side of the phone, but he seemed genuine. Two laptops arrived the next day.

By afternoon, a council chairman met me with his first suggestion. The food should not be doled out by the contractor. The cook should prepare it and then the council, on its own initiative, would arrange to carry the food to each tent. I told them that they were now an elected council. They should not come to me. They could talk to the kitchen contractor and the UNHCR on their own. The evening meal was thus distributed by the refugees themselves, at each tent, with minimal fuss. Then the council asked whether they could set up a reception stall of their own at the camp gate. On this, I was more than willing to help and put my money in their hands. The next day, the camp dwellers had set up a few chairs and a table with juice cartons and water jugs near the entrance, adjacent to the retired jihadis from Punjab.

This is the small difference between a shop run by servants and one run by its rightful owners.

Our state has always been run by its servants.

The first batch of civil and military bureaucrats of the new Pakistan took it upon itself to take this country to its rightful destiny, to rescue it from its 'corrupt and incompetent' owners—its elected representatives. The same elected representatives who were, through legislative and electoral victories, able to carve a new country out of the belly of mother India were defeated by the machinations of unelected government servants. Mohammad Ali Jinnah, the father of our nation, could feel this coming encroachment and half a year into the creation of the country, he addressed the elite officers' cadre of the military at the Staff College at Quetta and read out—*twice*—their oath that they were subservient to elected officials.

The first Pakistani cabinet was made up of men who had all been elected from some constituency, at least once in their lives. All, except one. The finance minister was not a democrat. The finance minister was a career government servant.

He was a Lahori. His name was Ghulam Muhammad.

But names are not important because the finance ministry then stayed in the hands of different government servants for the next twenty-five years, until 1971.

Five years after the country was made, four years after the death of Jinnah, the first government servant maneuvered his way into the presidency as well. The presidency, too, then stayed in the hands of these pen-pushers until 1971.

Soon after annexing the presidency, government servants then targeted the Ministry of Defence, which then also stayed under bureaucratic control until the country was finally broken, in 1971.

Thus, within eleven years of its formation, the entire cabinet was transformed from elected representatives to salarymen; these salarymen later also inducted some notables into the cabinet, who would become elected in the coming generations. But the original adherents of Jinnah's vision disappeared from the national scene—or began asking for a separate Bangladesh.

The eventual break up of the country in 1971 was so traumatic, so gruesome that elected representatives were finally handed control of both sides of the country. These suddenly elected representatives, spawned from the marriage of dictatorship and revolution, did not really understand their powers. Before they could learn to exercise these powers judiciously, they were again sent packing—their prime minister hanged. Wise, old, salaried men took over once again and held close these reins of power through to the end of the Cold War. After the end of the Cold War, the reins of power were loosened by salaried men. They started allowing elections but would field their favourite politicians and finance their favourite parties, and topple governments by judicial decrees or with military force as and when required.

In 2009, when I stood in Malakand trying to convince an elected representative that he was the owner and the blue-eyed commissioner the servant, the new member of the provincial assembly on the other side of the line was justified in not believing me. Sixty years of history had taught him the opposite.

When I was born in 1971, remember, my father too was a government servant. My father's father, the renowned eye surgeon in Gojra, worked for the government. All the brothers of my father who were of working age, whether they were engineers or doctors, worked for the government. Pakistan's top hockey players—gold medallists and world champions—were all government servants. The man who had broken the world record in hammer throw was a Pakistani government servant. The country's cricket stars all worked for government departments or corporations. The greatest squash player ever, a man who dominated his sport more than any other sportsman in history, worked for a government airline. Government was Big.

And it was about to become bigger. The first democratically elected government nationalized all private colleges and factories. Suddenly refinery managers, cotton spinners, professors, steel workers, all became government servants.

By the time the Cold War was over, the country had morphed into a bureaucrat's wet dream. The government did everything. The railway ran its own schools. The army ran its own farms. The food department ensured we had food. The Rice Corporation managed our rice. The Ministry of Industries owned tractor plants, chemical factories, refineries, textile units, cement factories and steel mills. The Ghee Corporation of Pakistan, for example, one of the ministry's many concerns, imported palm oil from Malaysia, routed it to dozens of factories, packaged it in tin cans, advertised its many brands, and ensured we had quality cooking oil for our homes. The government owned the largest banks in the country. Government servants thus doled out loans not only to other government corporations but also to any favoured politician who wanted to become a businessman or to a businessman who wanted to become a politician. These government banks thus spawned, through mega loans—later written off—a new crop of political families.

The era since the end of the Cold War has seen many of these government factories and banks sold out, but the struggle to wrest control of the country from the hands of government servants is still the seminal struggle of this country in every facet of life. Everything we know today has been coloured by the hands of government servants.

Because the government educated us, we have been brainwashed. We have been taught that elected representatives are evil. We firmly believe that the country was run aground by politicians—saved only through timely interventions by government servants. Our textbooks teach us that governments kept failing, forcing the military to take over time and time again. They do not tell us that salaried bureaucrats who sat in the presidency and in the Ministry of Defence and in the Ministry of Finance conspired and then fired these governments during the brief initial period when the country first tried fighting this fight at its very inception.

Then the government servant started putting his considerable mind around the very concept of Pakistan. Why was it created? Why did it have to be protected? How was a Pakistani different from an Indian? These issues were very simply answered by an ideology of Pakistan. This ideology, crafted by bureaucrats in the ministry of information, simply stated that Pakistan was created to defend Islam. Once created, the ideology was gifted with its chief defender, the army of Pakistan. These, though, were all artificial arguments we readily lapped up as schoolchildren and then firmly believed as adults.

This ideology had many holes. It is not polite to discuss them and treasonous to write about them. But the ideology has holes.

Firstly, we never asked what the ideology of Brazil or of Argentina or, for that matter, of India was. If Pakistan was created on the basis of Islam, the Indians could have said that they were made on the basis of Hinduism. Why did they not make that their ideology? Because they did not feel the need to explain India to Indians.

Secondly, when the country was split into two equally Islamic countries, we did not ask what the ideology of Bangladesh would now be. The two-nation theory, the basis of the ideology of Pakistan, was now effectively a three-nation theory and religion played second fiddle to nationalism. This split of the country in 1971 appears in our textbooks only as a quaint anecdote, a trivial sideshow. In reality, it was the largest massacre of a civilian Muslim population by any army in the modern era.

If that massacre did not flush the ideology of Pakistan into the Bay of Bengal, I do not know what will.

Lastly, I have always wondered, when the country was split into two countries, why did Bangladesh not claim rights to the name Pakistan? It was the larger country, after all. They should have been called Pakistan and we should have been called Punjabidesh. Why was the split termed a secession, not a divorce? Was it because the Bengalis had liberated themselves from the government servants of Pakistan, whereas the rest of us were destined to continue in our slavery for a few decades more?

After writing and then defending the ideology of Pakistan, government servants set about defining our identity. They quickly decided that different provinces with different languages could not make a nation. Doing the mathematics, they quickly arrived at the conclusion that Islam therefore had to be our identity. Only Islamic heroes then could be our heroes, they thought. This was then injected into our books.

As a result, Bhagat Singh, who gave his life in Lahore for the freedom of Lahore, could not be a hero. But Ahmad Shah Abdali, who sacked Lahore multiple times on his way to sacking Delhi, became our hero because he was a Muslim. Our Gakkhars, who fought against Afghan invaders, became villains and the Afghan invaders of yore who happened to be Muslim became heroes. The Jats and Rajputs of the Punjab (your ancestors) who fought the Mughals became villains and the Mughals who were the Muslim rulers of Delhi became heroes. Among the Mughals, Aurangzeb Alamgir, the most religious and the last of the great Mughals, became a superhero. His ancestor Akbar, the greatest of the Mughals, became a villain because he tried to launch a new religion combining Islam with Hinduism.

We did not adequately learn that the Indus Valley, present-day Pakistan, was the first civilization known to man. Seven thousand years ago, before the Egyptians, the Chinese or the Iraqis, we were the first civilization: a country of two thousand towns up and down the Indus, with cities as large as two hundred thousand inhabitants, with paved roads and drainage systems and grain stores and a written language and of course with bureaucrats, with trading ships snaking down the Indus to Iraq and to Kerala. But we are instead ashamed of this pre-Islamic past.

I distinctly remember a scholarly exchange in ninth grade where our Islamiyat teacher elaborated that there were those among us who dug up our past in archaeological sites and proudly show dug-up idols, ancient statues to the world and explain that our ancestors were sinners. Instead of burying this awful past, our teacher explained, these people were shockingly proud of their idol-worshipping ancestors.

Saeed Ejaz, otherwise a good boy, somehow was able to counter this airtight argument. He raised his hand and quoted a verse from the Quran that one must walk upon the earth and find out about one's ancestors. Our Islamiyat teacher was very impressed by Saeed's challenge and his eyes lit up in counterargument. The Quranic injunction, he underlined on the blackboard, explicitly directs one to walk upon the earth, not to go digging it up.

Such was our state of mind and such will be yours too. But I assure you we have legitimate heroes among us, if we only open our minds.

Karachi had the first airport of Asia. In 1960, the only Asian country other than Japan that manufactured its own metal-cutting lathe was Pakistan. We were able to launch a rocket into space in 1962. We pioneered television in Asia and have constructed the world's largest dams and its highest roads.

Punjab University has the honour of being associated with three Nobel laureates, the most in South Asia. We have never heard about the two pre-Partition laureates because they were not Muslim. The third, Abdus Salam, got his Nobel Prize as a Pakistani, but his name cannot be mentioned in polite conversation because his brand of Islam is not approved in Pakistan.

We now look at all heroes and villains through this government-sanctioned lens. Malala Yousafzai is considered a heroine all over the world, but in Pakistan the majority population is hesitant to call her so because she stands very clearly against a movement that professes Islamic foundations.

Similarly, the Talibanized rebels who are constantly attacking us are perversely considered heroes by us because they bear Islamic flags; subconsciously, we have been trained to believe that anyone who carries an Islamic flag is a supporter of the ideology of Pakistan, of Pakistan itself.

Afghanistan is the ideological frontier, where the fight for this ideology is actually taking place and this fight therefore must be won. If you ask any Pakistani he will tell you that Afghanistan has never been conquered. It is, in our minds, a mythical land. I was reminded of this when you, explaining to me your fourth-grade geography lesson, lit up while discussing Afghanistan. You were proud of it and you wanted to become it, because 'Afghanistan has never been conquered,' you said. I was perturbed by your hero-worship of everything Afghan because I too was taught the same thing despite the fact that in my lifetime I have never really seen a free Afghanistan.

I thought it was necessary for you to know that Alexander was not defeated in Afghanistan. He met his final match here in Pakistan. His historians record that all along the Indus River, his armies faced resistance, but it was on the banks of the Jehlum that Raja Porus—again unfortunately from our pre-Islamic past—fought Alexander to at least a draw, if not a defeat. The results of that famous battle are disputed, but it is not disputed that Alexander finally turned around and started back towards Greece after this battle—after burying his famous horse at Phalia in Pakistan.

Our pre-Islamic roots have been so trammelled that most families genuinely believe they came to the subcontinent with Muslim invaders and were never themselves invaded, and that their DNA is intrinsically different from the Hindus and Sikhs who cohabited these lands with them before Pakistan became Pakistan.

Our family distinctly remembers its Sikh roots and though I have no record of it I am sure we must have been Hindus before we were Sikhs. The same will be the case for most Pakistanis when we eventually take off the slog of ideology.

An ideology of Pakistan is not required to explain Pakistan. Nor can Islam, after the massacre of Bangladesh, any longer justify Pakistan. We are an accident of history like all the other nations on this planet. Like Argentina, or Brazil, we do not need a reason to be. We just are.

This fact does not take away from us the noble struggle for freedom. It only states simply that the Pakistan we know today was not formed in 1947. It was formed in 1971, the year I was born.

That year, before classes could break for spring vacation in Lahore, a column of tanks lined up in Dacca University in the middle of the night. While the cream of Bengal's future intelligentsia slept, the barrels were aimed at the hostel. A cold bureaucratic missive was transmitted. The tanks opened fire.

Seven months later, today's Pakistan was born.

Our majority does not know of this. We were innocent then because we did not know, but we are guilty now because we do not ask. We cannot bring back the past but we can at least understand the present.

I do not wish for you to feel ashamed because you had nothing to do with this, but I do wish for you to know what has passed so you can better command the future. Most of all, I wish for you to find your own identity and not to let government servants decide who you are.

Be not afraid. You can have an identity even now—in this new world—an identity you do not have to create only to recognize.

We all live with each other. No other people in this world live in close proximity to so many humans, with little electricity, some representation, a lot of guns, music, humour, Islam and hope. If we look hard, we can identify a Pakistani anywhere.

We are the grit and wile of a short and stocky Miandad as he constantly irks the six-foot Lillee until Lillee loses his temper and Miandad swings his bat at him in defiance. We are the same Miandad who swings and misses an Ian Botham outswinger again and again. Botham keeps repeating the same ball again and again and Miandad keeps swinging at it again and again. Both eye each other again and again. Eventually Miandad miscues and gets out, but that is who we are. Then, on another pitch, completely within the rules of the game, Srikanth thinks the ball he has played is dead and carelessly leaves his crease, only to see Miandad sauntering toward a ball still in play, picking it up and running him out. Srikanth storms off the field only to be invited back to play again. Not allowed, says the Umpire, but this has never happened in cricket—before or since.

We are the quiet grace of Hassan Sardar as he snaked his body and his hockey stick and the ball through five defenders to defeat India in India. We are the mythic picture conjured by a lonely radio commentator as the ball flies instantly from a wiry Hanif to the brothers Kalim and Salim at right-out to left-out in Buenos Aires and in Rome as we brought down team after team to get gold after gold.

We are the small-town confidence of the silver-medal team who threw their medals to the ground when the referee robbed them of their gold against Germany. We do not turn the other cheek. Yes, this is what we are.

We are also the lilt of Rafi and the swing of Kishore and the jhankar of Bollywood. Bollywood is as much a part of us as it is a part of India. There is no need to deny this. Lahore, when it is allowed, will add much needed style and pizzazz and a lot of flash to Bollywood for we are, at root, fashionable, artistic, poetic people, able to present complex thoughts in simple, body-shaking rhythms. We move with drums and live through music. Our languages ooze rhythm and the world is being mesmerized on dance floors globally by the beat of this country.

We are the heat of June and the dust of the time when the buffaloes come home. We are the smell of bread when it first hits the fire. We are the passion and love that resonates through the naked nights of summer.

We are snide remarks that do not require a response. We are the humour that carries us sanely across bomb blasts and sudden rushes to get home after a killing.

We are the skill of the metal worker in Gujranwala and of the ship breaker in Gadani. We are the nerve of the driver who keeps half a tyre suspended in air as he manoeuvers the passage of two jeeps on lonely mountain tracks. We love our technicians. The biggest form of praise we bestow is to say that someone is very technical. We love ingenuity. We love the earth and the metal with which we cut it.

We love water. We go crazy in the rain and sensually plough into the cold mouth of a running tube well. And we are always smiling. We are patient. We have the ability to coolly accommodate an idiot who has gone the wrong way in the middle of rush hour. We adapt to change.

We have faith in the big guy in the sky and we are always optimistic. We are supremely open-minded. We do not shun new ideas and we roll with what we have. This is the prime reason I say, tell us. Tell us that the ideology of Pakistan was just a bureaucratic cover. Tell us that the two-nation theory no longer works. Tell us what happened in Bangladesh. Tell us truthfully what is happening today in FATA and Afghanistan. And we will adapt and reconfigure and forgive and reboot.

A time will come when they will reluctantly tell us.

Until then, make do with what I am telling you. And trust me. We will recover. And we will then transform—from the brand name of terror—to one happening *qaum*.